Get Ready!

FOR STANDARDIZED TESTS

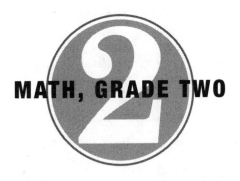

MATH, GRADE TWO

Other Books in the *Get Ready!* Series:

Get Ready!

FOR STANDARDIZED TESTS

MATH, GRADE TWO

Kristin B. Swanson

Carol Turkington
Series Editor

McGraw-Hill

New York   Chicago   San Francisco
Lisbon   London   Madrid   Mexico City
Milan   New Delhi   San Juan   Seoul
Singapore   Sydney   Toronto

Library of Congress Cataloging-in-Publication Data

Get ready! for standardized tests. Math.
    p. cm.—(Test preparation series)
  Includes bibliographical references.
  Contents: [1] Grade 1 / Sandy McConnell—[2] Grade 2 / Kristin Swanson
  ISBN 0-07-137399-3 (pbk. : v. 1)—ISBN 0-07-137400-0 (pbk. : v. 2)
  1. Mathematics—Study and teaching (Elementary)—United States.
2. Mathematics—Study and teaching—Parent participation—United States.   3. Achievement
tests—United States—Study guides. I. McConnell, Sandy. II. Test preparation series
(McGraw-Hill Companies)

  QA135.6 .G47   2001
  372.7—dc21   2001030901

McGraw-Hill

A Division of The McGraw·Hill Companies

1 2 3 4 5 6 7 8 9 0 COU/COU 0 9 8 7 6 5 4 3 2 1

ISBN 0-07-137400-0

This book was set in New Century Schoolbook by Inkwell Publishing Services.

Printed and bound by Courier.

McGraw-Hill books are available at special quantity discounts to use as premiums
and sales promotions, or for use in corporate training programs. For more information, please write to the Director of Special Sales, McGraw-Hill, Professional
Publishing, Two Penn Plaza, New York, NY 10121-2298. Or contact your local book-
store.

For Gene, Thomas, Adam, and Benjamin who love me no matter what, and for the 230 assorted second graders who have taught me so much.

K. S.

Contents

SKILLS CHECKLIST

MY CHILD ...	HAS LEARNED	IS WORKING ON
NUMERALS		
VERTICAL ADDITION		
FACT FAMILIES		
WORD PROBLEMS		
ADDENDS		
NUMERATION		
PLACE VALUE		
ORDINAL NUMBERS		
NUMBER PATTERNS		
EVEN NUMBERS		
ODD NUMBERS		
SYMBOLS		
SKIP COUNTING		
EXPANDED NOTATION		
TWO-DIGIT ADDITION		
TWO-DIGIT SUBTRACTION		
TELLING TIME		
CALENDARS		
MONEY		
MEASUREMENT		
GEOMETRY		
FRACTIONS		
MULTIPLICATION		
DIVISION		
PROBABILITY		
GRAPHS		

Introduction

Almost all of us have taken standardized tests in school. We spent several days bubbling-in answers, shifting in our seats. No one ever told us why we took the tests or what they would do with the results. We just took them and never heard about them again.

Today many parents aren't aware they are entitled to see their children's permanent records and, at a reasonable cost, to obtain copies of any information not protected by copyright, including testing scores. Late in the school year, most parents receive standardized test results with confusing bar charts and detailed explanations of scores that few people seem to understand.

In response to a series of negative reports on the state of education in this country, Americans have begun to demand that something be done to improve our schools. We have come to expect higher levels of accountability as schools face the competing pressures of rising educational expectations and declining school budgets. High-stakes standardized tests are rapidly becoming the main tool of accountability for students, teachers, and school administrators. If students' test scores don't continually rise, teachers and principals face the potential loss of school funding and, ultimately, their jobs. Summer school and private after-school tutorial program enrollments are swelling with students who have not met score standards or who, everyone agrees, could score higher.

While there is a great deal of controversy about whether it is appropriate for schools to use standardized tests to make major decisions about individual students, it appears likely that standardized tests are here to stay. They will be used to evaluate students, teachers, and the schools; schools are sure to continue to use students' test scores to demonstrate their accountability to the community.

The purposes of this guide are to acquaint you with the types of standardized tests your children may take; to help you understand the test results; and to help you work with your children in skill areas that are measured by standardized tests so they can perform as well as possible.

Types of Standardized Tests

The two major types of group standardized tests are *criterion-referenced tests* and *norm-referenced tests*. Think back to when you learned to tie your shoes. First Mom or Dad showed you how to loosen the laces on your shoe so that you could insert your foot; then they showed you how to tighten the laces—but not too tight. They showed you how to make bows and how to tie a knot. All the steps we just described constitute what is called a *skills hierarchy:* a list of skills from easiest to most difficult that are related to some goal, such as tying a shoelace.

Criterion-referenced tests are designed to determine at what level students are performing on various skills hierarchies. These tests assume that development of skills follows a sequence of steps. For example, if you were teaching shoelace tying, the skills hierarchy might appear this way:

1. Loosen laces.
2. Insert foot.
3. Tighten laces.
4. Make loops with both lace ends.
5. Tie a square knot.

Criterion-referenced tests try to identify how far along the skills hierarchy the student has progressed. There is no comparison against anyone else's score, only against an expected skill level. The main question criterion-referenced tests ask is: "Where is this child in the development of this group of skills?"

Norm-referenced tests, in contrast, are typically constructed to compare children in their abilities as to different skills areas. Although the experts who design test items may be aware of skills hierarchies, they are more concerned with how much of some skill the child has mastered, rather than at what level on the skills hierarchy the child is.

Ideally, the questions on these tests range from very easy items to those that are impossibly difficult. The essential feature of norm-referenced tests is that scores on these measures can be compared to scores of children in similar groups. They answer this question: "How does the child compare with other children of the same age or grade placement in the development of this skill?"

This book provides strategies for increasing your child's scores on both standardized norm-referenced and criterion-referenced tests.

The Major Standardized Tests

Many criterion-referenced tests currently in use are created locally or (at best) on a state level,

and there are far too many of them to go into detail here about specific tests. However, children prepare for them in basically the same way they do for norm-referenced tests.

A very small pool of norm-referenced tests is used throughout the country, consisting primarily of the Big Five:

- California Achievement Tests (CTB/McGraw-Hill)
- Iowa Tests of Basic Skills (Riverside)
- Metropolitan Achievement Test (Harcourt-Brace & Company)
- Stanford Achievement Test (Psychological Corporation)
- TerraNova [formerly Comprehensive Test of Basic Skills] (McGraw-Hill)

These tests use various terms for the academic skills areas they assess, but they generally test several types of reading, language, and mathematics skills, along with social studies and science. They may include additional assessments, such as of study and reference skills.

How States Use Standardized Tests

Despite widespread belief and practice to the contrary, group standardized tests are designed to assess and compare the achievement of groups. They are *not* designed to provide detailed diagnostic assessments of individual students. (For detailed individual assessments, children should be given individual diagnostic tests by properly qualified professionals, including trained guidance counselors, speech and language therapists, and school psychologists.) Here are examples of the types of questions group standardized tests are designed to answer:

- How did the reading achievement of students at Valley Elementary School this year compare with their reading achievement last year?

- How did math scores at Wonderland Middle School compare with those of students at Parkside Middle School this year?

- As a group, how did Hilltop High School students compare with the national averages in the achievement areas tested?

- How did the district's first graders' math scores compare with the district's fifth graders' math scores?

The fact that these tests are designed primarily to test and compare groups doesn't mean that test data on individual students isn't useful. It does mean that when we use these tests to diagnose individual students, we are using them for a purpose for which they were not designed.

Think of group standardized tests as being similar to health fairs at the local mall. Rather than check into your local hospital and spend thousands of dollars on full, individual tests for a wide range of conditions, you can go from station to station and take part in different health screenings. Of course, one would never diagnose heart disease or cancer on the basis of the screening done at the mall. At most, suspicious results on the screening would suggest that you need to visit a doctor for a more complete examination.

In the same way, group standardized tests provide a way of screening the achievement of many students quickly. Although you shouldn't diagnose learning problems solely based on the results of these tests, the results can tell you that you should think about referring a child for a more definitive, individual assessment.

An individual student's group test data should be considered only a point of information. Teachers and school administrators may use standardized test results to support or question hypotheses they have made about students; but these scores must be used alongside other information, such as teacher comments, daily work, homework, class test grades, parent observations, medical needs, and social history.

Valid Uses of Standardized Test Scores

Here are examples of appropriate uses of test scores for individual students:

- Mr. Cone thinks that Samantha, a third grader, is struggling in math. He reviews her file and finds that her first- and second-grade standardized test math scores were very low. Her first- and second-grade teachers recall episodes in which Samantha cried because she couldn't understand certain math concepts, and mention that she was teased by other children, who called her "Dummy." Mr. Cone decides to refer Samantha to the school assistance team to determine whether she should be referred for individual testing for a learning disability related to math.

- The local college wants to set up a tutoring program for elementary school children who are struggling academically. In deciding which youngsters to nominate for the program, the teachers consider the students' averages in different subjects, the degree to which students seem to be struggling, parents' reports, and standardized test scores.

- For the second year in a row, Gene has performed poorly on the latest round of standardized tests. His teachers all agree that Gene seems to have some serious learning problems. They had hoped that Gene was immature for his class and that he would do better this year; but his dismal grades continue. Gene is referred to the school assistance team to determine whether he should be sent to the school psychologist for assessment of a possible learning handicap.

Inappropriate Use of Standardized Test Scores

Here are examples of how schools have sometimes used standardized test results inappropriately:

- Mr. Johnson groups his students into reading groups solely on the basis of their standardized test scores.

- Ms. Henry recommends that Susie be held back a year because she performed poorly on the standardized tests, despite strong grades on daily assignments, homework, and class tests.

- Gerald's teacher refers him for consideration in the district's gifted program, which accepts students using a combination of intelligence test scores, achievement test scores, and teacher recommendations. Gerald's intelligence test scores were very high. Unfortunately, he had a bad cold during the week of the standardized group achievement tests and was taking powerful antihistamines, which made him feel sleepy. As a result, he scored too low on the achievement tests to qualify.

The public has come to demand increasingly high levels of accountability for public schools. We demand that schools test so that we have hard data with which to hold the schools accountable. But too often, politicians and the public place more faith in the test results than is justified. Regardless of whether it's appropriate to do so and regardless of the reasons schools use standardized test results as they do, many schools base crucial programming and eligibility decisions on scores from group standardized tests. It's to your child's advantage, then, to perform as well as possible on these tests.

Two Basic Assumptions

The strategies we present in this book come from two basic assumptions:

1. Most students can raise their standardized test scores.

2. Parents can help their children become stronger in the skills the tests assess.

This book provides the information you need to learn what skill areas the tests measure, what general skills your child is being taught in a particular grade, how to prepare your child to take the tests, and what to do with the results. In the appendices you will find information to help you decipher test interpretations; a listing of which states currently require what tests; and additional resources to help you help your child to do better in school and to prepare for the tests.

A Word about Coaching

This guide is *not* about coaching your child. When we use the term *coaching* in referring to standardized testing, we mean trying to give someone an unfair advantage, either by revealing beforehand what exact items will be on the test or by teaching "tricks" that will supposedly allow a student to take advantage of some detail in how the tests are constructed.

Some people try to coach students in shrewd test-taking strategies that take advantage of how the tests are supposedly constructed rather than strengthening the students' skills in the areas tested. Over the years, for example, many rumors have been floated about "secret formulas" that test companies use.

This type of coaching emphasizes ways to help students obtain scores they didn't earn—to get something for nothing. Stories have appeared in the press about teachers who have coached their students on specific questions, parents who have tried to obtain advance copies of tests, and students who have written down test questions after taking standardized tests and sold them to others. Because of the importance of test security, test companies and states aggressively prosecute those who attempt to violate test security—and they should do so.

How to Raise Test Scores

Factors that are unrelated to how strong students are but that might artificially lower test scores include anything that prevents students from making scores that accurately describe their actual abilities. Some of those factors are:

- giving the tests in uncomfortably cold or hot rooms;
- allowing outside noises to interfere with test taking; and
- reproducing test booklets in such small print or with such faint ink that students can't read the questions.

Such problems require administrative attention from both the test publishers, who must make sure that they obtain their norms for the tests under the same conditions students face when they take the tests; and school administrators, who must ensure that conditions under which their students take the tests are as close as possible to those specified by the test publishers.

Individual students also face problems that can artificially lower their test scores, and parents can do something about many of these problems. Stomach aches, headaches, sleep deprivation, colds and flu, and emotional upsets due to a recent tragedy are problems that might call for the student to take the tests during make-up sessions. Some students have physical conditions such as muscle-control problems, palsies, or difficulty paying attention that require work over many months or even years before students can obtain accurate test scores on standardized tests. And, of course, some students just don't take the testing seriously or may even intentionally perform poorly. Parents can help their children overcome many of these obstacles to obtaining accurate scores.

Finally, with this book parents are able to help their children raise their scores by:

- increasing their familiarity (and their comfort level) with the types of questions on standardized tests;
- drills and practice exercises to increase their skill in handling the kinds of questions they will meet; and

- providing lots of fun ways for parents to help their children work on the skill areas that will be tested.

Test Questions

The favorite type of question for standardized tests is the multiple-choice question. For example:

1. The first President of the United States was:

    A Abraham Lincoln

    B Martin Luther King, Jr.

    C George Washington

    D Thomas Jefferson

The main advantage of multiple-choice questions is that it is easy to score them quickly and accurately. They lend themselves to optical scanning test forms, on which students fill in bubbles or squares and the forms are scored by machine. Increasingly, companies are moving from paper-based testing to computer-based testing, using multiple-choice questions.

The main disadvantage of multiple-choice questions is that they restrict test items to those that can be put in that form. Many educators and civil rights advocates have noted that the multiple-choice format only reveals a superficial understanding of the subject. It's not possible with multiple-choice questions to test a student's ability to construct a detailed, logical argument on some issue or to explain a detailed process. Although some of the major tests are beginning to incorporate more subjectively scored items, such as short answer or essay questions, the vast majority of test items continue to be in multiple-choice format.

In the past, some people believed there were special formulas or tricks to help test-takers determine which multiple-choice answer was the correct one. There may have been some truth to *some* claims for past tests. Computer analyses of some past tests revealed certain biases in how tests were constructed. For example, the old advice to pick *D* when in doubt appears to have been valid for some past tests. However, test publishers have become so sophisticated in their ability to detect patterns of bias in the formulation of test questions and answers that they now guard against it aggressively.

In Chapter 1, we provide information about general test-taking considerations, with advice on how parents can help students overcome testing obstacles. The rest of the book provides information to help parents help their children strengthen skills in the tested areas.

Joseph Harris, Ph.D.

Test-Taking Basics

At some point during the 12 years that your children spend in school, they'll face a standardized testing situation. Some schools test every year, and some test every other year—but at some point your child will be assessed. How well your child does on such a test can be related to many things—did he get plenty of rest the night before? Is she anxious in testing situations? Did he get confused when filling in the answer sheets and make a mechanical mistake?

That's why educators emphasize that a child's score on a standardized test shouldn't be used as the sole judge of how that child is learning and developing. Instead, the scores should be evaluated as only one part of the educational picture, together with the child's classroom performance and overall areas of strength and weakness. Your child won't pass or fail a typical standardized test, but often you can see a general pattern of strengths and weaknesses.

What This Book Can Do

This book is not designed to help your child artificially inflate his scores on a standardized test. Instead, it's to help you understand the typical kinds of skills taught in a second-grade class and what a typical second grader can be expected to know by the end of the second year. It also presents lots of fun activities that you can use at home to work with your child in particular skill areas that may be a bit weak.

Of course, this book should not be used to replace your child's teacher but as a guide to help you work together with the school as a team to help your child succeed. Keep in mind, however, that endless drilling is not the best way to help your child improve. While most children want to do well and please their teachers and parents, they already spend about 7 hours a day in school. Extracurricular activities, homework, music, and play take up more time. Try to use the activities in this book to stimulate and support your children's work at school, not to overwhelm them.

Most children entering the second grade are eager to learn. One of the most serious mistakes that many parents of children this age make is to try to get their children to master skills for which they aren't developmentally ready. For example, while most children this age are ready to read, some aren't—and no amount of drill will make them ready to read.

There's certainly nothing wrong with working with your child, but if you're trying to teach the same skill over and over and your child just isn't "getting it," you may be trying to teach something that your child just isn't ready for.

Remember, however, that not all children learn things at the same rate. What may be typical for one second grader is certainly not typical for another. You should use the information presented in this book in conjunction with school work to help develop your child's essential skills in mathematics and number skills.

How to Use This Book

There are many different ways to use this book. Some children are quite strong in certain math areas but need a bit of help in other areas. Perhaps your child is a whiz at adding but has more trouble with telling time. Focus your attention on those skills which need some work, and spend more time on those areas.

You'll see in each chapter an introductory explanation of the material in the chapter, followed by a summary of what a typical child in second grade should be expected to know about these skills by the end of the year.

This is followed in each chapter by an extensive section featuring interesting, fun, or unusual activities you can do with your child to reinforce the skills presented in the chapter. Most use only inexpensive items found around the home, and many are suitable for car trips, waiting rooms, and restaurants.

Next, you'll find an explanation of how typical standardized tests may assess these skills and what your child might expect to see on a typical test.

We've included sample questions at the end of each section that are designed to help familiarize your child with the types of questions found on a typical standardized test. These questions do *not* measure your child's proficiency in any given content area—but if you notice that your child is having trouble with a particular question, you can use this information to figure out what skills you need to focus on.

Basic Test-Taking Strategies

Sometimes children score lower on standardized tests because they approach testing in an inefficient way. There are things you can do before the test—and that your child can do during the test—to make sure he does as well as he can.

There are a few things you might want to remember about standardized tests. One is that they can only ask a limited number of questions dealing with each skill before they run out of paper. On most tests, the total math component is made up of about 60 items and takes about 90 minutes. In some cases, your child may encounter only one exercise evaluating a particular skill. An important practice area that is often overlooked is the *listening* element of the tests. Most of the math questions are done as a group and are read to the students by the proctor of the test, who is almost always the classroom teacher.

You can practice this by reading the directions to each question to your second grader. Sometimes the instructions are so brief and to the point that they are almost too simple. In some cases, teachers are not permitted to reword or explain—they may only read what is written in the test manual. Read the directions as they have been given on the practice pages, and then have your child explain to you what they mean. Then you'll both be clear about what the tests actually require.

Before the Test

Perhaps the most effective thing you can do to prepare your child for standardized tests is to be patient. Remember that no matter how much pressure you put on your children, they won't learn certain skills until they are physically, mentally, and emotionally ready to do so. You've got to walk a delicate line between challenging and pressuring your children. If you see that your child isn't making progress or is getting frustrated, it may be time to lighten up.

Don't Change the Routine. Many experts offer mistaken advice about how to prepare children for a test, such as recommending that children go to bed early the night before or eat a high-protein breakfast on the morning of the test. It's a better idea not to alter your child's routine at all right before the test.

If your child isn't used to going to bed early, then sending him off at 7:30 p.m. the night before a test will only make it harder for him to get to sleep by the normal time. (Of course, you should try not to keep your child up too late.) If he is used to eating an orange or a piece of toast for breakfast, forcing him to down a platter of fried eggs and bacon will only make him feel sleepy or uncomfortable.

During the Test

There are some approaches to standardized testing that have been shown to make some degree of improvement in a score. Discuss the following strategies with your child from time to time.

Neatness. There is an incorrect way to fill in an answer sheet on a standardized test, and if this happens to your child, it can really make a difference on the final results. It pays to give your child some practice on filling in answer sheets. Watch how neatly your child can fill in the bubbles, squares, and rectangles below. If he overlaps the lines, makes a lot of erase marks, or presses the pencil too hard, try having him practice with pages of bubbles. You can easily create sheets of capital O's, squares, and rectangles that your child can practice filling in. If he gets bored doing that, have him color in detailed pictures in coloring books or complete connect-the-dots pages.

Bring Extra Pencils. You don't want your child spending valuable testing time jumping up to sharpen a pencil. Send along plenty of extra, well-sharpened pencils, and your child will have more time to work on test questions.

Listen Carefully. You wouldn't believe how many errors kids make by not listening to instructions or not paying attention to demonstrations. Some children mark the wrong form, fill in the bubbles incorrectly, or skip to the wrong section. Others simply forget to put their names on the answer sheets. Many make a mark on the answer sheet without realizing whether they are marking the right bubble.

Read the Entire Question First. Some children get so excited about the test that they begin filling in bubbles before they finish reading the entire question. The last few words in a question sometimes give the most important clues to the correct answer.

Read Carefully. In their desire to finish first, many children tend to select the first answer that seems right to them without thoroughly reading all the responses and choosing the very best answer. Make sure your child understands the importance of evaluating all the answers before choosing one.

Skip Difficult Items; Return Later. Many children will sit and worry about a hard question, spending so much time on one problem that they never get to problems that they would be able to answer correctly if they only had left enough time. Explain to your child that he can always come back to a knotty question once he finishes the section.

Refer to Pictures for Clues. Tell your child not to overlook the pictures in the test booklets, which may reveal valuable clues that children can use to help them find the correct answers. Students also can find clues to correct answers by looking at descriptions, wording, and other information from the questions.

Use Key Words. Have your child look at the questions and try to figure out the parts that are important and those which aren't.

Eliminate Answer Choices. Just like in the wildly successful TV show *Who Wants to Be a Millionaire,* remind your child that it's a good idea to narrow down the choices among multiple-choice options by eliminating answers he knows can't possibly be true.

Try Guessing. It's okay to guess—some children (especially high achievers) won't guess because they don't want to put down a poten-tially wrong answer. This is true even if they can eliminate some of the choices. Make sure, there-fore, that your child knows that in this case it's okay to guess.

Nobody's Perfect. Reassure your child that he won't be expected to know all the answers. There will be some items that are too difficult—that's just how these tests are designed. Sometimes when children (especially high achievers) find some questions they don't know the answer to, they become extremely anxious and upset that they don't know something they "should" know.

On to the Second Chapter

Now that you've learned a bit about the test-taking basics, it's time to turn your attention to the first of the math skills—number basics.

CHAPTER 2

Basic Facts

When elementary school teachers talk about *basic facts,* they're referring to single-digit addition problems and subtraction problems from 0 to 18. For example, $0 + 0 =$___ or $9 + 9 =$___, and $1 - 1 =$___ or $18 - 9 =$___; these math problems can't be figured out by writing them down—children are expected to just "know them."

It takes a lot of practice, but eventually, your child shouldn't have to use her fingers or a number line. Math facts should become second nature. Children at the end of second grade should be able to answer them as quickly as they would say their own names. That's the idealistic goal. Realistically, only about half of all second graders know their basic facts this well. If your child is struggling with the mastery of basic facts, there are lots of things you can do to help her.

What Second Graders Should Know

Children in second grade should have a beginner's math vocabulary and be able to use it when solving problems. Some of these words are

- *set*
- *add*
- *value*
- *subtract*
- *sum*
- *difference*
- *solve*
- *math sentences*
- *fact families or related facts*
- *missing addend*

These words should be familiar and make sense when your child reads them in directions. Children this age also should be able to match number words with numerals and sets of objects, and add and subtract by interpreting pictures. Word problems or story problems ask children to read a short scenario and then compose the math sentence that best solves the problem. There is also a timed element that accompanies basic facts. Since children should know their facts "by heart," they are expected to be able to complete a certain number of problems in a set amount of time.

Recently, more emphasis has been placed on the *processes* involved in math in addition to the answers. Children are being asked to explain in a written sentence *why* they chose a certain answer or *how* they arrived at a specific solution. This doesn't come easily for most youngsters. However, it's a skill that's being taught in schools and required on many types of assessments, including some new standardized tests.

Many children aren't sure how or why an answer makes sense to them—it "just does." By talking about the steps they followed in solving a problem, children learn to communicate their thought processes verbally and, eventually, in writing.

What You and Your Child Can Do

Count Everything in Sight! You may think your second grader is too big for counting, but she will be expected to understand the meaning of some very large numbers. The best time is when you're stuck at a railroad crossing. We've counted trains with 140 cars! While driving, count cars in the other lane, buildings, billboards, streetlights, telephone poles, and so on.

Practice. Practice basic addition and subtraction facts any time, anywhere, but have a predictable system in mind. Start with doubles, such as $2 + 2$, $5 + 5$, $8 + 8$, $12 - 6$, $14 - 7$, $6 - 3$, etc. This is a good warmup strategy that builds confidence. Then move to facts of 10, like $7 + 3$, $4 + 6$, $8 + 2$, $10 - 5$, $10 - 9$, $10 - 6$ and ask your child over and over until you feel that she is secure. Continue with facts for each number (for example, $4 + 5$, $8 + 1$, $6 + 3$, and $7 + 2$ all equal 9, so ask them together). Mix the facts as your child improves, asking "tricky" facts every other time.

Flash Cards. Flash cards are great and can help improve speed, but they shouldn't be the only thing you use to practice. Be aware that some flash cards are two-sided and have the answer printed in a tiny corner as a related fact. Children train themselves to rely on these instead of really looking at the problem itself.

Roll the Dice! Get a pair of dice and play a math game by adding the numerals on each. Or choose a higher number such as 12, roll one of the dice, and subtract the numeral shown.

Play Cards. Use the same idea as the dice game, but liven it up by fanning out the cards and, in your best magician's voice, saying, "Pick a card, any card!" This is especially helpful when practicing three-addend math problems.

Oh, Domino! Playing dominoes helps children visualize a number and then match the numeral. Dominoes can be added or subtracted but are most helpful when practicing fact families or related facts.

Go for a Drive. Look at the route numbers, speed limit signs, and other street signs, and turn them into math problems. On a drive to Grandma's, the route number may be 568, so the math problem would be $5 + 6 + 8 = $ ___. When you turn onto Rt. 309, the problem becomes $3 + 0 + 9 = $ ___.

Take a Walk. Make up story problems as you take your walk. "There are six kids riding their bikes. How many would there be if four of them had to go home for lunch?" "Here comes a line of eight cars. Here come three more. How many cars just passed us?"

Build Houses. This activity helps with fact families (related facts). Using blocks, modeling clay, or Legos, build three houses. Use numbers on cards or plastic magnet numbers, and put one in two of the houses. Ask, "If you added those numbers, who would live in the next house?" "If you subtracted the numbers, where would the numbers move?" "What signs would be in the yards, plus, minus, or equals?"

What's in the Basket? For this you can use a small basket, bag, box, or other container. Use some sort of counter, such as buttons, pennies, marbles, blocks, or M&Ms, and (secretly) put a few in the bag. Show a few on the table. Tell your child the total number, and let her figure out the number in the bag. "If we have 8 on the table and there are 13 all together, how many must be in the bag?" This is fun if you're waiting in a long line and you have a pocket full of change. Hold out a few coins in your hand, tell your child the total—she'll tell you how many are in your pocket.

What Tests May Ask

A standardized test may ask any number of questions dealing with basic facts, but time and space on the test limit the number of items pertaining to one particular concept. Tests also account for children who are working below grade level and therefore include problems that students should have mastered in first grade. Your child should be prepared to perform the following tasks:

- Count objects and choose the matching numeral.
- Match a picture to a corresponding math problem.
- Identify related facts or fact "families" (such as $3 + 4 = 7$, $7 - 4 = 3$, $4 + 3 = 7$, and $7 - 3 = 4$).
- Add and subtract basic facts.
- Find the missing addend: $6 + \underline{} = 14$.
- Read a story problem, choose the accompanying math problem (including which operation to use, addition or subtraction), and solve it. These may include two-step problems as well.

Practice Skill: Numerals

Directions: Choose the numeral that shows how many.

Example:

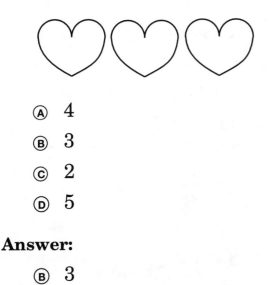

- Ⓐ 4
- Ⓑ 3
- Ⓒ 2
- Ⓓ 5

Answer:

- Ⓑ 3

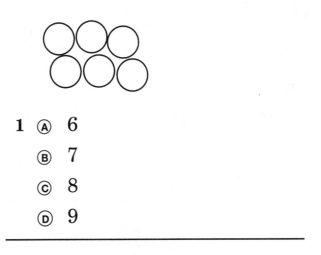

1 Ⓐ 6

Ⓑ 7

Ⓒ 8

Ⓓ 9

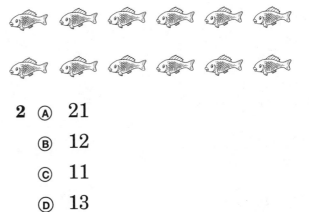

2 Ⓐ 21

Ⓑ 12

Ⓒ 11

Ⓓ 13

3 Ⓐ 3

Ⓑ 4

Ⓒ 5

Ⓓ 6

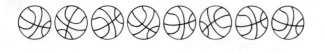

4 Ⓐ 12

Ⓑ 5

Ⓒ 17

Ⓓ 8

5 Ⓐ 15

Ⓑ 51

Ⓒ 16

Ⓓ 14

(See page 101 for answer key.)

Practice Skill: Vertical Addition

Directions: Choose the math problem that shows what is happening in the picture below.

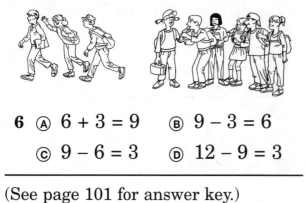

6 Ⓐ $6 + 3 = 9$ Ⓑ $9 - 3 = 6$

Ⓒ $9 - 6 = 3$ Ⓓ $12 - 9 = 3$

(See page 101 for answer key.)

Practice Skill: Fact Families

Directions: Which math fact belongs to the fact family shown?

Example:

$2 + 3 = 5$
$5 - 3 = 2$
$5 - 2 = 3$

Ⓐ $5 + 3 = 8$

Ⓑ $3 + 2 = 5$

Ⓒ $5 - 1 = 4$

Ⓓ $3 - 2 = 1$

Answer:

Ⓑ $3 + 2 = 5$

7 $6 + 5 = 11$
$11 - 5 = 6$
$11 - 6 = 5$

Ⓐ $11 + 5 = 16$

Ⓑ $6 - 5 = 1$

Ⓒ $5 + 6 = 11$

Ⓓ $11 - 4 = 7$

8 $4 + 9 = 13$
$9 + 4 = 13$
$13 - 9 = 4$

Ⓐ $3 + 4 = 7$

Ⓑ $9 - 4 = 5$

Ⓒ $5 + 4 = 9$

Ⓓ $13 - 4 = 9$

9 $5 + 8 = 13$
$8 + 5 = 13$
$13 - 5 = 8$
Ⓐ $13 - 8 = 5$ Ⓑ $13 - 13 = 0$
Ⓒ $8 - 5 = 3$ Ⓓ $13 + 5 = 18$

Directions: Choose the related fact.

Example:

$10 + 3 = 13$
Ⓐ $10 - 10 = 0$ Ⓑ $13 - 3 = 10$
Ⓒ $3 - 3 = 0$ Ⓓ $3 + 0 = 3$

Answer:

Ⓑ $13 - 3 = 10$

---

10 $14 - 7 = 7$
Ⓐ $7 + 7 = 14$
Ⓑ $7 - 7 = 0$
Ⓒ $14 - 4 = 10$
Ⓓ $7 + 0 = 7$

---

11 $9 + 8 = 17$
Ⓐ $9 - 8 = 1$
Ⓑ $17 - 7 = 10$
Ⓒ $9 + 9 = 18$
Ⓓ $17 - 8 = 9$

---

12 $3 + 4 = 7$
Ⓐ $7 + 3 = 10$
Ⓑ $7 - 3 = 4$
Ⓒ $4 + 7 = 11$
Ⓓ $7 - 0 = 7$

Directions: Match the fact family to the picture shown below.

13 Ⓐ $5 + 5 = 10$ $10 - 5 = 5$

Ⓑ $7 + 5 = 12$ $5 + 7 = 12$
$12 - 5 = 7$ $12 - 7 = 5$

Ⓒ $12 - 10 = 2$ $12 - 2 = 10$
$2 + 10 = 12$ $10 + 2 = 12$

Ⓓ $10 - 7 = 3$ $10 - 3 = 7$
$7 + 3 = 10$ $3 + 7 = 10$

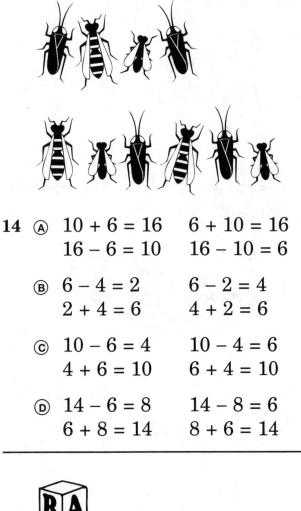

Directions: Read and solve the following problems.

Example:

Heta had three candies. She ate them all. How many does she have left?

- Ⓐ $3 + 0 = 3$
- Ⓑ $3 - 3 = 0$
- Ⓒ $0 + 3 = 3$
- Ⓓ $0 - 0 = 0$

Answer:

- Ⓑ $3 - 3 = 0$

---

14 Ⓐ $10 + 6 = 16$ $6 + 10 = 16$
$16 - 6 = 10$ $16 - 10 = 6$

Ⓑ $6 - 4 = 2$ $6 - 2 = 4$
$2 + 4 = 6$ $4 + 2 = 6$

Ⓒ $10 - 6 = 4$ $10 - 4 = 6$
$4 + 6 = 10$ $6 + 4 = 10$

Ⓓ $14 - 6 = 8$ $14 - 8 = 6$
$6 + 8 = 14$ $8 + 6 = 14$

16 James caught 5 butterflies. He let them all go. How many does he have now?

- Ⓐ $5 + 5 = 10$
- Ⓑ $5 - 5 = 0$
- Ⓒ $10 - 5 = 5$
- Ⓓ $5 - 0 = 5$

---

15 Ⓐ $3 - 2 = 1$ $3 - 1 = 2$
$1 + 2 = 3$ $2 + 1 = 3$

Ⓑ $3 - 3 = 0$ $3 - 0 = 3$
$3 + 0 = 3$ $0 + 3 = 3$

Ⓒ $3 + 3 = 6$ $6 - 3 = 3$

Ⓓ $3 + 2 = 5$ $2 + 3 = 5$
$5 - 3 = 2$ $5 - 2 = 3$

17 Carlitos walked 3 blocks to Jane's house and then 5 more blocks to the store. How many blocks did Carlitos walk?

- Ⓐ $5 - 3 = 2$
- Ⓑ $3 + 2 = 5$
- Ⓒ $3 + 5 = 8$
- Ⓓ $8 - 3 = 5$

18 Which word in question 17 helped you to know which problem to choose?

Ⓐ *walked*

Ⓑ *blocks*

Ⓒ *more*

Ⓓ *many*

19 Markku has 9 baseball cards. Eddie has 5 baseball cards. How many more cards does Markku have than Eddie?

Ⓐ 9 + 5 = 14

Ⓑ 14 − 5 = 9

Ⓒ 14 − 9 = 5

Ⓓ 9 − 5 = 4

20 Xiang Yi and Ben had a race. Ben crossed the finish line in 15 seconds. Xiang Yi crossed the finish line in 9 seconds. How many seconds faster was Xiang Yi than Ben?

Ⓐ 15 − 9 = 6

Ⓑ 15 + 9 = 21

Ⓒ 9 + 6 = 15

Ⓓ 6 + 6 = 12

21 Kris had 7 flowers in her hand. She gave 5 flowers to her Daddy. Now how many flowers does Kris have?

Ⓐ 7 − 5 = 2

Ⓑ 7 − 2 = 5

Ⓒ 7 + 5 = 12

Ⓓ 12 − 5 = 7

(See page 101 for answer key.)

Practice Skill: Addends

Directions: Find the missing addends in the following problems.

Example:

$5 + \underline{} = 6$

Ⓐ 0

Ⓑ 1

Ⓒ 4

Ⓓ 6

Answer:

Ⓑ 1

22 $8 + \underline{} = 15$

Ⓐ 5

Ⓑ 9

Ⓒ 7

Ⓓ 11

23 $4 + \underline{} = 12$

Ⓐ 16

Ⓑ 10

Ⓒ 6

Ⓓ 8

24 $7 + \underline{} = 13$

    Ⓐ 6

    Ⓑ 5

    Ⓒ 4

    Ⓓ 3

25 $\underline{} + 3 = 11$

    Ⓐ 14

    Ⓑ 4

    Ⓒ 9

    Ⓓ 8

26 $\underline{} + 5 = 14$

    Ⓐ 9

    Ⓑ 19

    Ⓒ 6

    Ⓓ 15

(See page 101 for answer key.)

CHAPTER 3

Numeration

As adults, we don't think of numeration as a skill to be learned. It's just part of our storehouse of knowledge, and we take for granted how it got there. But young children are novices when it comes to numeration. Second graders receive a lot of practice in school with these number concepts, including

- place value
- ordinal numbers
- odd and even numbers
- greater than and less than
- skip-counting
- expanded notation

What Second Graders Should Know

By the end of the year, your child will know a lot about numeration; it will become second nature to him, just like it is for you. For example, if you show him a three-digit numeral such as 425, he should know that the 4 is in the hundreds place and equals 400, the 2 is in the tens place and equals 20, and the 5 is in the ones place and equals 5. If you line up some magic markers, he should know which color is the third in line, the fifth, the eleventh, and so on.

Skip-counting helps kids see number patterns and sets the stage for multiplication, which in some schools is taught (although not usually mastered) in second grade. Odd and even numbers are introduced in this grade, but it takes practice to keep them straight. Estimating helps

children understand approximate values and comprehend that math isn't always an exact science.

By the end of the year, your child will be expected to understand the vocabulary of numeration and be able to relate information regarding each when shown examples. The vocabulary includes

> *ones place*
>
> *tens place*
>
> *hundreds place*
>
> *number order*
>
> *skip-counting*
>
> *odd and even numbers*
>
> *estimating*
>
> *number patterns*
>
> *greater than (>) and less than (<)*

What You and Your Child Can Do

On the Road Again! As you drive along life's highways and byways, your children can be learning math skills. As you head down I-95, talk about in which "place" each number lives (tens or ones). Read billboards and street addresses as you drive or walk, and ask the value of the numbers you read:

YOU: Route 724! What's the value of the 7?

CHILD: 700.

YOU: That's terrific!

Little Houses Redux. Remember the little houses we built in the last chapter? Use them again, but label them *hundreds, tens,* and *ones.* Ask who is living in which house and what is the value of the number. What if the numbers move around and trade places? What are the values then?

A Variation on a Theme. Use the same houses, but turn them into garages and put masking tape numbers on some little matchbox cars. Ask:

"What is the value of the 5 if it's parked in the tens garage?" (50)

"What numeral will we get if we combine the 7 in the hundreds garage, the 5 in the tens garage, and the 2 in the ones garage?" (752)

Line Up! Your child's toys will help a lot in many of the practice activities, and they also make math work seem more like playtime. Line up stuffed animals, plastic soldiers, cars, books, dolls, baseball cards, crayons, and so on. Point to one, and ask your child its position in line (Fifth? Eighth?), or ask your child to point to the ninth car or the fifteenth book. Spice it up by moving or removing objects to see how fully he understands the concept.

Don't Put the Toys Away Yet. The same friends used in the previous ordinal number exercise will help with skip-counting. Number the objects with masking tape or sticky notes, and move them toward your child if they are being counted or away from him if they are being skipped.

Skip It! Get out your jump rope and count the jumps in lots of different ways, by 2s, 5s, and 10s, and don't forget hundreds! (Kids love counting these huge numbers.)

Skipping Again? To show skip-counting in higher numbers, use a 10×10 block grid numbered 1 to 100. Use pennies or counters to cover some of the numbers (every fifth number, every tenth number, etc., and observe the patterns you

form together. Or you can set up the pattern and ask your child to tell you about it. What pattern does he see? These ideas apply to odd and even patterns as well.

Oddball. This time we'll use smaller manipulatives, such as buttons, dried beans, or the ever-popular jelly beans! Any kind of candy is a great incentive and is fun to handle. M&M's, Skittles, Swedish fish, or candy corn works well. If you don't have much of a sweet tooth, Cheerios, pretzel nubs, or grapes are just fine. Start with a small handful, and count them first. Maybe you'll have 13. Ask your child to make pairs and put the pairs in a line. Hey! There's one left over. That's the oddball, so 13 is an odd number. Try it again with 16. This time there is no oddball, everyone has a partner, so 16 is an even number. Make a list of the odd and even numbers. It shouldn't take too long to see that even numbers always end with a 0, 2, 4, 6, or 8 in the ones place.

"Big Mouth!" No offense. It's just the name of a neat way to practice "greater than" and "less than." Take a paper plate and cut out a wedge equaling one-quarter of the plate. The opening is the mouth of "Big Mouth." Your child can draw eyes and hair to spruce him up a bit. On paper, a white board, or the sidewalk in chalk (a big favorite), write two numbers, leaving a plate-sized space between them. Remind your child that "Big Mouth" eats the biggest number he can find. Turn the mouth to "eat up" the greater number, and then discuss what the matching math sentence would sound like. For example, "Thirty-five is less than fifty-nine."

An Educated Guess. Estimating makes children a little uneasy. They've been trained to respond to math questions with precise answers. After all, 2 + 2 = 4, not 5 or "about 3." There is only one right answer. Estimating asks children to "think outside the box," which also takes training. For this exercise, get a few different sized containers ranging from as small as a film canister to as big as a gallon jug—and a bunch of others in between. Using a spoon and sand, rice, dirt, or even water (if you're patient), start filling the containers. Have your child guess how many scoops it will take to fill the containers. Then let him play. Inevitably, he will try filling larger containers using the smaller ones. He will be estimating without even knowing it.

Hop to It! Make a long masking tape number line on the floor, sidewalk, or driveway. Help your child to evenly space the numbers from 0 to about 50. Circle the 10, 20, 30, 40, and 50 with red. Take turns placing an object on the number line and telling which ten it is closest to. Then put it in a sentence. For example, "Twenty-seven is about thirty."

Goodie Jars. Remember the munchies mentioned in the game oddball? Fill some small transparent containers with some, and have your child estimate the number inside. Remind him to look at the bottom and count (the best he can) what he sees. That number will help him estimate. The closest guess gets to keep the goodies! This also works with bunches of things like pencils and stacks of things like collectible cards.

What Tests May Ask

Standardized tests strive to measure a child's ability, no matter how weak or how sophisticated. Numeration items on these tests will ask children to recall first-grade concepts, solve second-grade problems, and attempt skills taught in higher-level math classes. These tests also will determine how well a child can think abstractly. Your child will be asked to show that he understands movement between numbers and that he can apply numeration principals.

The tests will ask children to

• Identify place value.

• Name the position of an object using ordinal numbers. (What color is the sixth flower?)

• Skip-count by 2s, 3s, 5s, 10s, and 100s and be able to identify patterns when viewing numerals in a sequence. Children should know how to fill in missing numbers in the pattern or continue the pattern. For example:

10, 15, 20, ___, 30, 35

or

20, 22, 24, 26, 28, ___, ___

• Identify odd numbers and even numbers.

• Show the value of a number in expanded notation (that is, $396 = 300 + 90 + 6$).

• Compare two numbers and determine which number is greater than or less than the other.

• Understand the meaning of the symbols <, >, and = in a number sentence.

• Estimate the approximate value of a number or a set.

Standardized tests ask children to answer questions in a bit of an unusual way, since they are rarely told to "fill in little circles as neatly and completely as possible."

Believe it or not, by completing the activity pages in this book, your second grader gets to practice this seemingly insignificant skill. Preparation of this sort may seem silly, but it goes a long way in making a student feel secure in a new testing situation. If your child can say, "Oh, I get it. I did this before," he'll feel much more comfortable. For this reason, we have sometimes provided the responses "Not here," "None of the above," and "NG" (not given) among the choices. Seen for the first time, these responses may rattle a 7- or 8-year-old, but practice leads to security.

Practice Skill: Numeration

Directions: Find the value of the underlined numeral.

Example:

2̲3

Ⓐ 2

Ⓑ 20

Ⓒ 200

Ⓓ NG (not given)

Answer:

Ⓑ 20

---

1 6**7̲**

Ⓐ 7

Ⓑ 70

Ⓒ 700

Ⓓ NG

---

2 **5̲**1

Ⓐ 5

Ⓑ 50

Ⓒ 500

Ⓓ 5

---

3 **4̲**39

Ⓐ 4

Ⓑ 40

Ⓒ 400

Ⓓ 4000

(See page 101 for answer key.)

Practice Skill: Place Value

Directions: Find the matching number in the following questions about place value.

Example:

8 tens, 2 ones.

Ⓐ 802

Ⓑ 28

Ⓒ 82

Ⓓ NG

Answer:

Ⓒ 82

---

4 5 tens and 6 ones.

Ⓐ 506

Ⓑ 56

Ⓒ 65

Ⓓ NG

---

5 8 hundreds, 0 tens, 3 ones.

Ⓐ 83

Ⓑ 38

Ⓒ 8003

Ⓓ 803

(See page 101 for answer key.)

Practice Skill: Ordinal Numbers

Directions: Look at the picture below and answer the questions about the picture.

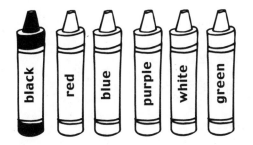

Example:

Which crayon is green?

Ⓐ sixth

Ⓑ third

Ⓒ first

Ⓓ second

Answer:

Ⓐ sixth

---

6 Which crayon is red?

Ⓐ third

Ⓑ fourth

Ⓒ second

Ⓓ sixth

---

7 Which crayon is purple?

Ⓐ first

Ⓑ fourth

Ⓒ third

Ⓓ sixth

---

8 What color is the first crayon?

Ⓐ black

Ⓑ orange

Ⓒ yellow

Ⓓ not here

---

9 What color is the fifth crayon?

Ⓐ pink

Ⓑ silver

Ⓒ green

Ⓓ white

(See page 101 for answer key.)

Practice Skill: Number Patterns

Directions: Look for a number pattern. Choose the answer that provides the missing number or numbers.

Example:

2, 4, 6, ___, 10

Ⓐ 5

Ⓑ 7

Ⓒ 8

Ⓓ 9

Answer:

Ⓒ 8

---

10 12, 14, 16, 18, ___, ___, ___
- Ⓐ 19, 20, 21
- Ⓑ 16, 14, 12
- Ⓒ 20, 22, 24
- Ⓓ 21, 24, 27

11 35, 40, 45, 50, ___, ___, ___
- Ⓐ 51, 52, 53
- Ⓑ 55, 60, 65
- Ⓒ 52, 54, 56
- Ⓓ 49, 48, 47

12 12, 15, 18, ___, 24, 27
- Ⓐ 19
- Ⓑ 20
- Ⓒ 21
- Ⓓ 25

13 50, 54, 58, 62, ___, 70, 74
- Ⓐ 63
- Ⓑ 64
- Ⓒ 65
- Ⓓ 66

(See page 101 for answer key.)

Practice Skill: Even Numbers

Directions: Choose the even number.

Example:
- Ⓐ 3
- Ⓑ 41
- Ⓒ 25
- Ⓓ 62

Answer:
- Ⓓ 62

14 Ⓐ 7
- Ⓑ 43
- Ⓒ 56
- Ⓓ 111

15 Ⓐ 8
- Ⓑ 19
- Ⓒ 25
- Ⓓ 627

16 Ⓐ 9
- Ⓑ 33
- Ⓒ 41
- Ⓓ 516

(See page 101 for answer key.)

Practice Skill: Odd Numbers

Directions: Choose the odd number.

Example:

- Ⓐ 40
- Ⓑ 11
- Ⓒ 26
- Ⓓ 62

Answer:

- Ⓑ 11

17 Ⓐ 2
- Ⓑ 25
- Ⓒ 28
- Ⓓ 280

18 Ⓐ 13
- Ⓑ 44
- Ⓒ 30
- Ⓓ 552

19 Ⓐ 12
- Ⓑ 212
- Ⓒ 211
- Ⓓ 112

20 Ⓐ 6
- Ⓑ 72
- Ⓒ 90
- Ⓓ NG

(See page 101 for answer key.)

Practice Skill: Symbols

Directions: Choose the symbol or number that makes the sentence true.

Example:

14 ___ 65

- Ⓐ <
- Ⓑ >
- Ⓒ =
- Ⓓ −

Answer:

- Ⓐ <

21 35 ___ 48
- Ⓐ <
- Ⓑ >
- Ⓒ =
- Ⓓ −

22 29 ___ 10

  Ⓐ   <

  Ⓑ   >

  Ⓒ   =

  Ⓓ   +

24 77 < ___

  Ⓐ   87

  Ⓑ   77

  Ⓒ   35

  Ⓓ   7

23 581 > ___

  Ⓐ   851

  Ⓑ   815

  Ⓒ   158

  Ⓓ   591

25 86 = ___

  Ⓐ   68

  Ⓑ   86

  Ⓒ   886

  Ⓓ   668

(See page 101 for answer key.)

CHAPTER 4

Two-Digit Addition and Subtraction

Much of the beginning of second grade is spent reviewing and refining skills learned in first grade. Then, sometime after the winter holidays in a typical school, teachers begin to introduce addition and subtraction of two- and three-digit numbers and teach the concept of "regrouping" or "renaming." When you were in school, your teacher probably called it "carrying" and "borrowing," and some teachers are going back to those little catch phrases because they make sense to children. At first it isn't a big deal, but for some children it can be the most frustrating thing they've ever attempted. It is important for parents to understand that the best way for children to learn math concepts is a hands-on approach. Children need to see things in a concrete way before they can comprehend them in their abstract form. Regrouping is a perfect example of this.

What Second Graders Should Know

Children in second grade will rely heavily on their understanding of place value when they begin this new skill. It is imperative that they know that 10 ones are the same as 1 ten and that 10 tens equal 1 hundred. This base-ten system is seen easily in our monetary structure, which is a good tool to use when practicing. Children need to understand that regrouping or renaming is just like making an even trade. They should know when it is and is not necessary to regroup or make a trade.

Once children master two-digit addition and subtraction, three-digit addition is added to the heap. This comes very easily for most second graders.

What You and Your Child Can Do

Standardized tests generally do very little to entertain their young consumers, although the newest ones have many more pictures than before. Still, it is a test—it's not supposed to be fun. But your practice time can be! There isn't a whole lot you can do to jazz up regrouping, but there are games you can teach your child that will pave the way to her understanding of the concepts needed.

Start with Models. Get a box or two of plastic straws or a bunch of craft sticks. You'll also need a few rubber bands. Bundle the sticks in tens, and leave a pile of ones. Use a tablet to write an addition or subtraction problem, and then ask your child to gather the models. Ask, "Do we need to regroup?" If you do, be sure you have 10 ones before you bundle them.

Try the same with subtraction. Begin with a problem, and then bundle the sticks to match the numbers you've chosen. Talk through the steps with your child, emphasizing "start with the ones column, decide whether or not to regroup, etc." If you need to regroup, open one of the bundles and show the trade.

This can be practiced using clear film canisters holding 10 of whatever you choose. Buttons, dried beans, M&M's, etc. can all be used as manipulatives to assist with your practice games.

"Fair Trade." Play this game with any standard deck of cards. Take out all the 10s and place them on the table; then remove all the face cards. Each player starts with two cards. Take turns drawing cards one at a time and discarding a card each time. The idea is to get cards that add up to 10. When you do, you get to trade for a 10. The player with the most 10s at the end of the game (no cards left in the drawing deck) *wins*!

Beanbags. On a piece of poster board, draw lines to make a nine-square grid. Write a different two-digit number on each square. Do the same on the other side using different numbers. Ask your child to toss two beanbags. Using the numbers on which the beanbags land, make up an addition or subtraction problem. Continue until all the numbers have been used.

Score! During basketball season, find a game on TV, and begin watching with your child. As the scores increase, watch for the score to come up in the corner of your screen. When it does, help your child to quickly write it down, higher number on top. Add the numbers first; then rewrite the problem and subtract. Ask, "How big is the lead?" The subtraction difference is the answer. Keep your remote control handy for this one—the chances of a 7-year-old maintaining interest in this for the entire game are slim. Feel free to "surf" in between!

Money Matters. Get out the loose change in your pocket. Put a few coins in one hand and a few in the other. Ask your child to count the money in one hand and write down the amount, then do the same for the other. Ask:

"How much do I have?"

"How much more is in this hand than in the other?"

Mix up the coins and try again.

Good Ol' Days. Children love to hear stories about when you were a kid. Tell them some of the things you remember (keep them positive, funny, light-hearted), and mix in two-digit numbers for them to calculate as you wax nostalgic! For example, "You're so lucky to get 75 cents when the tooth fairy visits you. When I was little, I was lucky to get a quarter! What's the difference between those amounts?" Or "I rode bus 63 to school, and you ride bus 19. What is the sum of those numbers?"

What Tests May Ask

Two-digit addition and subtraction is a math computation skill and is included in that portion of the test. Your child will be asked simply to solve the problems in a certain amount of time and probably to solve some word problems involving two-digit numerals as well. Children will be expected to do the following:

- Identify numbers by looking at models.

- Combine sets of models.

- Add two- and three-digit numbers without regrouping.

- Subtract two- and three-digit numbers without regrouping.

- Add two- and three-digit numbers with regrouping.

- Subtract two- and three-digit numbers with regrouping.

- Solve word problems using two-digit addition and subtraction with and without regrouping.

- Solve problems on scratch paper and transfer the solution to the test page.

Practice Skill: Adding and Subtracting

Directions: Choose the correct answer for each question below.

Example:

23
+51

- Ⓐ 64
- Ⓑ 74
- Ⓒ 63
- Ⓓ 73

Answer:

- Ⓑ 74

1 31
+42

- Ⓐ 46
- Ⓑ 37
- Ⓒ 73
- Ⓓ NG

2 82
+11

- Ⓐ 102
- Ⓑ 93
- Ⓒ 39
- Ⓓ 71

3 20
+49

- Ⓐ 69
- Ⓑ 29
- Ⓒ 96
- Ⓓ 25

4 25
+26

- Ⓐ 78
- Ⓑ 41
- Ⓒ 1
- Ⓓ 51

5 47
+36

- Ⓐ 11
- Ⓑ 71
- Ⓒ 73
- Ⓓ 83

6 46
+ 8

- Ⓐ 44
- Ⓑ 84
- Ⓒ 42
- Ⓓ 54

7 71 + 41 = ___

 Ⓐ 32

 Ⓑ 30

 © 112

 Ⓓ 85

8 83 + 21 = ___

 Ⓐ 62

 Ⓑ 52

 © 104

 Ⓓ NG

9 47 + 31 = ___

 Ⓐ 78

 Ⓑ 18

 © 16

 Ⓓ 76

10 53 − 44 = ___

 Ⓐ 9

 Ⓑ 11

 © 97

 Ⓓ 91

11 40 − 16 = ___

 Ⓐ 36

 Ⓑ 24

 © 26

 Ⓓ 47

12 92 − 26 = ___

 Ⓐ 74

 Ⓑ 78

 © 56

 Ⓓ 66

13 123 + 123 = ___

 Ⓐ 66

 Ⓑ 200

 © 36

 Ⓓ 246

14   856
  +143

 Ⓐ 713

 Ⓑ 137

 © 371

 Ⓓ 999

15   359
  + 20

 Ⓐ 339

 Ⓑ 361

 © 559

 Ⓓ 379

16 Kim has 45 books. Mike has 45 books, too. How many books do they have all together?

Ⓐ 85

Ⓑ 80

Ⓒ 90

Ⓓ 99

17 Ned brought 32 cupcakes to school. He and his classmates ate 28 of them. How many cupcakes did he take back home with him?

Ⓐ 6

Ⓑ 4

Ⓒ 60

Ⓓ NG

18 The toy store had 85 yo-yos. It sold 42 of them. How many yo-yos are left?

Ⓐ 43

Ⓑ 47

Ⓒ 63

Ⓓ 36

19 Rob blew up 26 balloons. Later, his friend Makoto helped him blow up 51 more balloons. How many balloons did they blow up?

Ⓐ 37

Ⓑ 35

Ⓒ 75

Ⓓ 77

20 Thi Len's big fish tank had 19 fish in it. She won 4 fish at the fair and put them in her tank. How many fish are in Thi Len's tank?

Ⓐ 15

Ⓑ 59

Ⓒ 23

Ⓓ 39

(See page 101 for answer key.)

CHAPTER 5

Time: Clocks and Calendars

Telling time is one of the most abstract and challenging math skills that second graders are expected to master. It combines several skills and requires children to think about the same numbers that they have just come to understand in a completely different way. At this level it includes minutes and hours, as well as calendar concepts like days and dates, weeks, months, and years. Add to this the digital age in which we live, and you can see why telling time and understanding concepts of time can be a source of anxiety for the children in our lives.

Think about it. There are 24 hours in a day, but only 12 on a clock. In all other math skills, 1 means 1, 2 means 2, 3 means 3—but when telling time, 1 means 1 some of the time, but sometimes it means 5. Two means 2 sometimes, and sometimes it means 10. And 3 can mean 3, 15, or a quarter! Digital clocks make it easy to confuse 2s and 5s, 6s and 9s, 4s and 9s, and 3s and 8s. Some months have 30 days and some have 31, and one only has 28, except once every 4 years, when it has 29. Whew!

In many ways, telling time depends on your child's developmental readiness. With most children, when they are ready, time just "clicks," and they get it. It's not automatic, but they will reach a point where the concepts really start to make sense.

What Second Graders Should Know

By the end of the second grade, children should know how to tell time to the nearest 5-minute interval on a face clock and to the minute on a digital clock. In some schools they may be required to know the 1-minute intervals on a face clock, too. The language of time is tricky and can cause some confusion. Second graders are just beginning to understand that 4:30, 30 minutes after 4, and half past four all mean the same thing. They should understand calendar concepts, including days of the week, months of the year, days in a month, and the difference between days and dates. An often unmentioned skill is the understanding of elapsed time, including earlier and later.

What You and Your Child Can Do

Talk about Time. For beginning second graders, increments of time can be quite elusive. Our novice time tellers often have a hard time determining how much time has passed and how long things take—hence the infamous phrase, "Are we there yet?" To give kids a better idea of the length of a minute, hour, and so on, talk about time as you do things together: "Let's make some cookies. How long will that take? Two minutes? Two hours? Two days?" Or, "We're going to visit the Spencers tonight. It will take 30 minutes or half of one hour to get there. What other things can you do in that amount of time?"

Just a Minute! This quick little activity helps children to grasp the concept of 1 minute in a hands-on way. Try these exercises (and more if you think of them) to see how many you can complete in 1 minute. Write them down, and next to each one make a prediction about how many you *think* can be done. Use a watch with a second hand to time your child. This works as a fun party game, too. How many times can you

• Write your name

• Sing the ABC's (keep a tally)

• Hop on one foot

• Clap your hands

• Touch your toes (all the way up; no cheating!)

• Count to 10 (keep a tally)

• Draw smiley faces

• Run up and down the stairs

• Throw a ball up in the air and catch it

• Click your tongue

Be Math-Minded. As mentioned at the beginning of this book, becoming "math-minded" is a really important part of preparing your child for math in the real world, as well as for standardized tests. Be sure you have a face clock that your child can manipulate somewhere in the house. It can be a kitchen clock, an alarm clock (these are a real hoot to play with!), or even a watch with a traditional face. It should have numbers, not lines or dots where the numbers belong. If you're thinking of buying a watch for your son or daughter, be math-minded, not fashion-minded. Make sure it has numbers and is easy to put on and take off. Some children's watches even show the 5-minute intervals (5, 10, 15, 20, etc.) in one color and the numbers 1 to 12 in another, and the minute and hour hands are colored to match.

Clock Watcher. Start talking about time as you go about your daily routine. Take a few extra seconds to show your child (on his watch or on another clock) what you mean. For instance, when you wake up in the morning, try this. "What time is it, Adam?" (6:30 a.m.) "We have to leave for school at 8:00. How much time do we have to get ready?" Or, "Your violin lesson is from 4:45 to 5:30. How long will we be there?" Or perhaps in a more frantic tone, "It's 7:55, and you still haven't brushed your teeth or made your bed. We're leaving in 5 minutes. What time are we leaving?"

TV Math. Save your TV listings, especially the pages that spread out the shows for an entire Saturday morning. Look at the chart together, and note which shows are 30 minutes (one half hour), 60 minutes (one hour), or more ("How many minutes would that be?"). Have your child color the 30-minute shows one color, the hour-long shows another, etc.

Double Talk. When talking about time with your child, get in the habit of telling time in several different ways. For example, if dinner is at 5:45, say, "Be home for dinner at 5:45, quarter of six, 45 minutes after 5:00, 15 minutes before 6." Have your child repeat one or two of the times. It might sound silly, but your second grader probably will think it's pretty funny and that you're playing a game.

What in the World? Get a map of the world, a globe, or even a road atlas with a U.S. map (another car activity!). Time zones or little clocks are usually printed across the top. Talk about time zones and the differences in time between states and countries. Ask your second grader, "If it is 2:20 here in Arizona, what time is it at Uncle Jason's house in Pennsylvania?" Or, "If we're having dinner here in New York, what are the people in Japan doing right now (besides making video games!)?"

Calendar Fun. Save your old calendars, or sometime in February or March (when calendars are dirt cheap), buy your child one of his own. Put family birthdays on it. Mark on it holidays that your family celebrates, upcoming vacations, dentist appointments, and other dates that directly involve your child. Discuss the days, dates, duration, and so on.

Time Machine. Pretend you're in a time machine. (For a super adventure, give your child a great big box—one he can fit inside. With markers, crayons, paper, and some glue, this can take days to decorate, or at least one rainy afternoon.) This activity really makes kids think. Ask your child if he can recall the event that you name. How far back will the time machine have to take us to get there? Five minutes, five hours, five days, or five years? For example, "Remember Ann's birthday party? How far back would the time machine take us to get back to that time? Two minutes, two days, two weeks, or two years?" Or, "When was your little sister born? Three hours ago, three days ago, three months ago, or three years ago?"

What Tests May Ask

Standardized tests won't use a lot of paper asking questions about time, but there will be some questions on this topic. Tests will show face clocks and digital clocks and ask children to choose the correct time, or they may show a clock and direct the students to "Mark the time that is 15 minutes earlier (or later) than the time shown." They will show calendars and ask questions about the information that can be found in a particular month (such as "On what day is October 10th?" or "What is the date of the third Sunday in June?"). The tests also will give word problems concerning elapsed time (such as "The movie started at 7:00 and ended at 9:00. How long was the movie?" or "I told Jan to come to my house at 3:00. She said she would be a half hour late. What time did she get to my house?").

Practice Skill: Telling Time

Directions: Choose the clock that shows the time given.

Example:

3:40

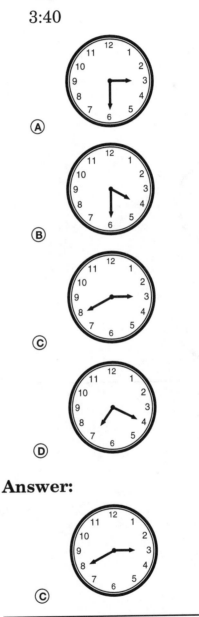

Ⓐ

Ⓑ

Ⓒ

Ⓓ

Answer:

Ⓒ

1 1:50

2 6:10

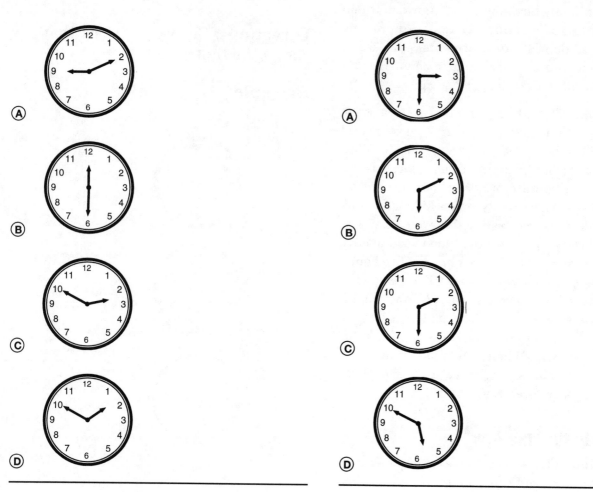

3 Half past 8

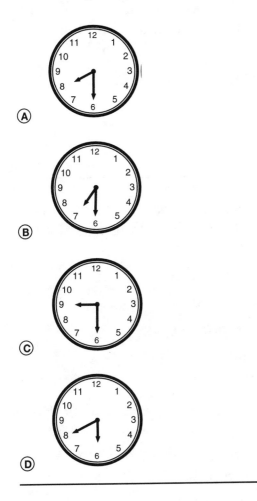

Ⓐ

Ⓑ

Ⓒ

Ⓓ

Answer:

Ⓐ 12:20

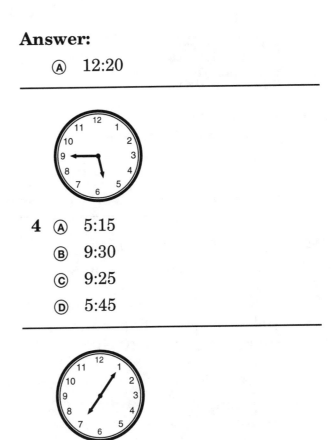

4 Ⓐ 5:15

Ⓑ 9:30

Ⓒ 9:25

Ⓓ 5:45

5 Ⓐ 1:30

Ⓑ 1:35

Ⓒ 7:05

Ⓓ 7:10

Directions: Choose the correct time that is shown on the clocks below.

Example:

Ⓐ 12:20

Ⓑ 4:00

Ⓒ 12:25

Ⓓ none of the above

6 Ⓐ nine o'clock

Ⓑ quarter past nine

Ⓒ half past nine

Ⓓ quarter to nine

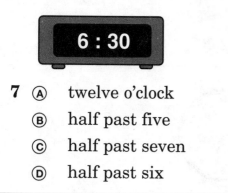

7 Ⓐ   twelve o'clock

  Ⓑ   half past five

  Ⓒ   half past seven

  Ⓓ   half past six

Directions: Read the following questions and choose the correct answer for each.

8 Choose the clock that shows 15 minutes *later than* 10:30.

9 Lin wants to have dinner at 5:00 p.m. She has to cook the ham for 3 hours. What time should she put the ham in the oven?

  Ⓐ   5:00

  Ⓑ   3:00

  Ⓒ   1:00

  Ⓓ   2:00

10 The show started at 7:30. It was over at 9:00. How long was the show?

  Ⓐ   30 minutes

  Ⓑ   60 minutes

  Ⓒ   90 minutes

  Ⓓ   100 minutes

11 Raye took her dog for a walk. She left at 4:10 and got home at 5:00. How long did Raye walk her dog?

  Ⓐ   50 minutes

  Ⓑ   10 minutes

  Ⓒ   70 minutes

  Ⓓ   1 hour

(See page 101 for answer key.)

38

Practice Skill: Calendars

Directions: Look at the calendar below to answer questions 12 through 16.

MAY

Sun.	Mon.	Tues.	Wed.	Thurs.	Fri.	Sat.
	1	2	3	4	5	6
7	8	9	10 Sue's birthday	11	12	13
14 Mother's Day	15	16	17	18	19 School picnic	20
21	22	23	24	25	26	27
28	29 Memorial Day	30	31			

12 How many days are there in the month of May?

Ⓐ 30

Ⓑ 31

Ⓒ 29

Ⓓ 28

13 On what day of the week is Mother's Day?

Ⓐ Monday

Ⓑ Friday

Ⓒ Saturday

Ⓓ Sunday

14 How many Fridays are there in May?

Ⓐ 2

Ⓑ 3

Ⓒ 4

Ⓓ 5

15 What is the date of the school picnic?

Ⓐ June 19

Ⓑ April 19

Ⓒ May 12

Ⓓ May 19

16 Sue's party is the Saturday after her birthday. When is Sue's party?

Ⓐ May 6

Ⓑ May 13

Ⓒ May 20

Ⓓ May 27

(See page 101 for answer key.)

CHAPTER 6

Money

Math concepts involving money are probably the only ones that you don't have to "bring to life" for your child. By age 7, children know the perks, importance, and power of money. They know that it puts food on the table, gas in the car, and shoes on their feet—well, sort of. For most second graders, money is what buys them collectible cards, a new skateboard, and computer games, and it's that stuff jingling in their pockets that they'd better not lose between home and the school cafeteria. In our largely cashless society, children often don't have the opportunity to actually see money changing hands, but they are expected to understand the value of currency in its many forms.

What Second Graders Should Know

One of the first things primary school students are taught about money is that there is no correlation between a coin's size and its value. This gets a bit complicated, in much the same way as the numbers on a clock in the last chapter. Children are secure in their counting skills using one-to-one correspondence, but to count money, they have to forget all about that and count certain little round things by ones, others by fives, others by tens, and those big ones by twenty-fives. When youngsters try to count them all mixed together, it can be discouraging. In addition to counting coins, second graders also should understand the equivalent values of coins. For instance, a 50-cent piece or half dollar = 2 quarters = 5 dimes = 10 nickels = 50 pennies.

They need to understand the place value of a written amount of money as well. This includes the ¢ and $ symbols and the number places in relation to the decimal point. Second graders are taught to "count up" from a given amount to one dollar in order to make change, but it is not a skill they have mastered at this level.

What You and Your Child Can Do

Skip-Counting. Practice skip-counting with a twist. Begin by reviewing skip-counting by fives and tens up to 100. Then go back and ask your child to count by fives starting with a multiple of five (randomly chosen by you). We'll use 35. Kids may need some help getting started, so you can count together, "35, 40, 45, 50, 55, 60, etc." up to 100. Do this several times so that your child feels comfortable counting by fives, starting anywhere. Do the same thing with tens. But this time you can start with any number at all and keep going. If you start with 23, your child would continue with 33, 43, 53, 63, etc. If you start with 9, your child would continue with 19, 29, 39, 49, etc.

Jingle, Jingle! Any time you have coins in your pocket or in your wallet, empty them out, and let your child "go to it!" This can become a daily routine that will solidify your child's confidence in counting money. Spread the coins out on a flat surface, and always begin by telling your child to line up the coins in order of their *value,* left to right, greatest to least. This first step will make things a lot easier.

Stop/Switch. In this game, you do the counting, but your second grader needs to pay very close attention to what you say. Start with a group of mixed coins arranged "in order" by your child, as mentioned above. *She* should remind *you* how to count each coin—quarters by twenty-fives, dimes by tens, nickels by fives, and pennies by ones. Then *you* start counting. When you first try the game, point to a coin each time you say an amount. When you both have the hang of it, stop pointing. Every time you get ready to change a counting pattern, your child should yell, "Stop! Switch." If she doesn't say "Stop! Switch!" keep going with the same pattern. If she says it at the right times, the total amount will be correct; if she doesn't, it will be wrong.

How Much More? Start with a pile of coins or a combination of bills and coins. Ask your second grader to count the money and write the total. Then think of a round number just above the total. Let's say you have $3.47. "How much more money would we need to make $3.50?" "How much more would we need to make $4?" "How about $5?" Use coins and bills to show the amount growing to reach the next total. When this skill gets easier for your child, remove the actual coins and try it just on paper, using the numerals and imagination.

Yard Sale. Clean up and clean out. Let your child enjoy this learning experience with you. Of course, you'll have to supervise, but the smaller "nickel and dime" items are a great tool to help your child understand earning and spending money. Let her help you make price tags before the sale and count the profits after. Go out for ice cream with the money you've made, and you'll have a budding economist on your hands in no time.

Strictly Business. There are lots of things a young person can do to earn money, from extra jobs around the house to helping neighbors. All these activities help strengthen a child's understanding of money concepts. But there's not a child around who wouldn't love to have her own "business." If you read *Arthur's Pet Business* by Marc Brown, your second grader will be inspired to try it herself. Brainstorm ideas together. Here are a few to get you started:

Lemonade stand

Homemade cookies

Pictures or paintings done by your child

Leaf raking

Snow shoveling

Dog walking

Weed pulling

Make signs to advertise, and let the fun begin!

What Tests May Ask

Only a page or two of most standardized tests are devoted to money. This boils down to about five to ten questions. Most of these will ask students to identify a set of coins that equals the amount shown, choose the amount that is represented by the picture shown, or choose an alternate way to make a given amount. Word problems are included, and one or two may ask about making change. Some tabulation will need to be done on scratch paper and then be transferred to the test page.

Practice Skill: Money

Directions: Choose the correct amount that is the same amount as the coins in the picture.

Example:

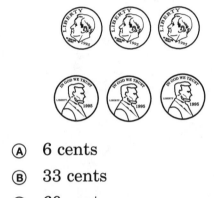

- Ⓐ 6 cents
- Ⓑ 33 cents
- Ⓒ 60 cents
- Ⓓ 78 cents

Answer:

- Ⓑ 33 cents

1 Ⓐ 3 cents
- Ⓑ 15 cents
- Ⓒ 30 cents
- Ⓓ 75 cents

2 Ⓐ 1 dollar
- Ⓑ 50 cents
- Ⓒ 80 cents
- Ⓓ 70 cents

3 Ⓐ 70 cents
- Ⓑ 66 cents
- Ⓒ 35 cents
- Ⓓ 73 cents

4 Ⓐ 51 cents
- Ⓑ 70 cents
- Ⓒ 35 cents
- Ⓓ 61 cents

Directions: Read the following questions and choose the correct answer for each.

5 Choose the group of coins that is worth the *least* amount of money.

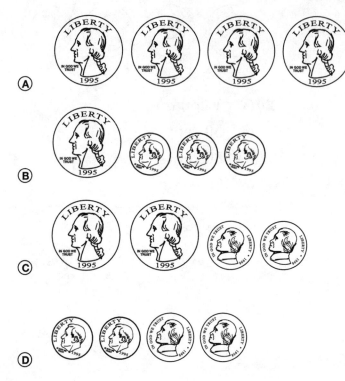

6 Choose the group of coins that is worth the *most* money.

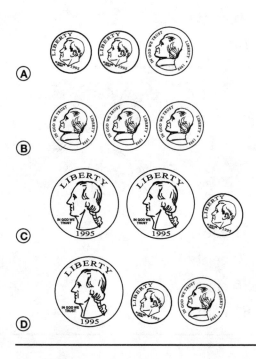

Directions: Look at the picture below to answer questions 7 and 8.

7 Greg has $1.00 in his pocket. Choose the item that he *cannot* buy.

(A)   (B)

(C)   (D)

8 Choose the two items that Greg could buy with his $1.00.

(A)

(B)

(C)

(D)

Directions: Read the following questions and choose the correct answer for each.

9 Lane has a half dollar. If she bought a lollipop for 35 cents, how much change would she get back?

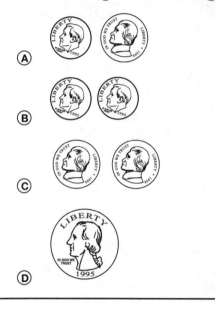

Ⓐ

Ⓑ

Ⓒ

Ⓓ

10 Amy has two quarters. David has three quarters. Eduardo has 10 dimes. Chinda has 8 nickels. Who has the most money?

Ⓐ Amy

Ⓑ David

Ⓒ Eduardo

Ⓓ Chinda

11 Thomas went to the store with one dollar bill and 2 quarters. Choose the item Thomas could buy with the money he has.

Ⓐ Super ball, $2.00

Ⓑ Race car, $1.85

Ⓒ Baseball cards, $1.40

Ⓓ Jump rope, $1.75

12 At a yard sale, Luz wanted to sell her marbles for 30 cents, her cars for 75 cents, and her Old Maid game for 50 cents. How much money will she get if she sells all three of these things?

Ⓐ $.90

Ⓑ $1.55

Ⓒ $1.50

Ⓓ $1.45

(See page 101 for answer key.)

CHAPTER 7

Measurement

An average second-grade classroom teacher will spend about three weeks introducing and practicing the many concepts of measurement found in the curriculum. These ideas will reappear as review items and in learning centers throughout the school year. But a standardized test probably will ask only five or six questions on the subject. Since we don't know which five skill areas the test will choose, it's important to know the basics of them all.

These include linear measurement using standard and metric systems, as well as the measurement of capacity, mass, area, perimeter, and temperature using both systems. You'll be very relieved to know that students at this level are not expected to know this vocabulary (although it may be mentioned in passing by some teachers) and even more relieved that second graders aren't expected to convert standard to metric and vice versa. Children in second grade may be asked to estimate an approximate distance, weight, or volume using metric or standard units of measurement, however. Thankfully, it's not nearly as confusing for kids as it may seem if it's presented in a simple way.

What Second Graders Should Know

There are a lot of ideas that are new to 7- and 8-year-olds on the subject of measurement. Here are some of the vocabulary words your child will know at the end of the year:

inch	*degrees Fahrenheit*
pint	*decimeter*
gallon	*gram*
centimeter	*yard*
liter	*quart*
perimeter	*meter*
area	*kilogram*
foot	*weight*
cup	

Children should know the meanings of these words and when each unit of measurement should be used. They also should know which "tool" to use and how to use it properly. For example, a pencil should be measured using inches or centimeters, but the playground could be measured in yards or meters. If you want to know how much a brick weighs, you should use pounds or kilograms. Equivalent measurements are taught and students should have an understanding of these. The metric system is actually easier to understand because it is a base-ten system. For example, 100 centimeters = 1 meter in the same way that 100 cents = 1 dollar. But children should still know that 2 cups = 1 pint and 2 pints = 1 quart; therefore, 4 cups = 1 quart, etc.

At this level, estimation is a large part of measurement, and it helps children to understand the difference between the units in both the standard and metric systems. For instance, if you needed a long piece of rope to hang a tire swing from a tree, would you need 10 inches of rope, 10 feet of rope, or 10 yards of rope? The same is true in measuring temperature. If it's hot enough to go swimming, is it about 0°C, 30°C, or 100°C? Of course, the best way to learn any of these concepts is to use them, and for children, using measurement tools is a lot like play.

What You and Your Child Can Do

Measurement is one area of math where you as a parent won't have to work very hard to make it "real." Children are naturally curious about the sizes and weights of the things in their world, especially really huge things like rockets and dinosaurs and extremely tiny things like seeds, bugs, and germs. They themselves are growing every day, and they love to see how tall they've gotten and how strong they are. The activities to practice measurement therefore will allow your child to make a personal connection as well as have a lot of fun.

Make It Personal. Start with your second grader and a big piece of butcher paper (you also can use the sidewalk or driveway). Whatever you decide to use, have your child lie down, and trace him in magic marker or chalk. Using a ruler, help him to measure the length of an arm, leg, neck, hand, foot, and fingers. Measure the width of his head, shoulders, and waist. Talk about which unit of measurement works best for each body part. You couldn't measure his pinky finger in feet, but centimeters would work perfectly. Then trade places, and let your child trace and measure you. Compare the sizes of your feet, hands, and overall height. Some parents may even be measured in yards! Be sure to date the drawings and hang them in your child's room, or roll them up and save them for viewing when your child has grown a bit.

Scavenger Hunt. Set up a trail of clues leading to different rooms in your house where your child can measure objects. List the item in each room that you want him to measure, or give him the dimensions and have him find the object and write it down. Here are some samples: "Go to the place where the goldfish swim, and measure the height of the thing they swim in." When your child gets to the aquarium, he can measure its height, jot it on his paper, and read the next clue. It might be, "When you go to the movies and sit in the theater, you might have this by the ounce or the liter." You also might have your child searching for box and container labels that show the contents in grams, kilograms, liters, etc. The possibilities are endless. By the way, your clues don't have to rhyme, unless you have a lot of time on your hands!

Sand, Water, Rice. These sound like the ingredients to a really bad recipe! You'll want to give your child some measuring cups and access to either water, a sand box, or a tub of rice. Rice works best because it's easiest to clean up, works in any season, and is perfect for measuring or just playing. Go to your nearest dollar store and grab a big storage tub with a snug lid, not smaller than about 6 gallons. Then, on your next trip to one of those superstores where you can get stuff in bulk, buy about 10 to 15 pounds of rice. It's pretty cheap when you buy a lot. You'll also want to hang onto your empty plastic containers (labels on if you can keep them intact and still get the container clean). Milk cartons, yogurt cups, margarine tubs, and plastic soda, juice, and shampoo bottles all work perfectly. Encourage your child to play with measuring cups and empty containers to determine equivalent units and to see what a certain amount really looks like. You'll have a tough time dragging your second grader (or any grader!) away from this project.

Brownies á la Mode. Baking brownies is a great way to incorporate many units of measurement into one terrific adventure. First, you need a brownie mix (of course, you can work from scratch if you want). Guide your child, but let him do most of the work himself. He'll need to preheat the oven (temperature), find the right size pan (9 × 13 inch, linear) and gather his ingredients. Ask him to read all the labels and tell the unit used. Then measure out the other ingredients (capacity) and mix them. He'll have to rely on his knowledge of time to be sure the brownies are properly baked. He could even cut them into 3-inch squares. (Á la mode is optional!)

What Tests May Ask

Most of the measurement questions asked on a standardized test will very likely show a picture of a measurement tool and ask the child to read what a certain object measures. For example, it might show a thermometer and ask, "What is the temperature shown?" Or it might show a ruler next to a stick and ask, "How long is this stick?"

This may sound really easy, and for most children, it is, once they understand how to use the tools. Remember, each measuring tool has its own "quirks." Most thermometers show incremental lines every 2 degrees and a number every 5 or every 10 degrees. Measuring cups come in sets where each cup is a different measurement, or liquid can be measured using one measuring cup where all the increments are included and are separated by lines. Rulers have standard units on one side and metric units on the other. A scale can be digital, or look like a face clock, or a balance. It's trickier than it seems.

Tests also usually will ask students to measure the perimeter of a shape or to determine the perimeter of a rectangle given the length of two of the sides. Other measurement questions may be in the form of a word or story problem. "If we're having a party and this is the punch recipe, how many quarts of punch will we have? 2 cups lemonade, 2 cups orange juice, 2 cups ginger ale, 1 cup pineapple juice, 1 cup apple juice." In addition, measurement concepts may be combined with other math skills in two- or three-step problems. "Rover weighs 28 pounds. Spot weighs 10 kilograms. Barkley's weight is some-where between that of Rover and Spot. Which weight could be Barkley's?"

Practice Skill: Measurement

Directions: What is the length of each object shown?

Example:

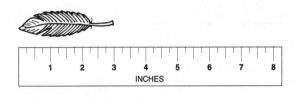

Ⓐ 3 centimeters

Ⓑ 3 inches

Ⓒ 3 feet

Ⓓ 3 yards

Answer:

Ⓑ 3 inches

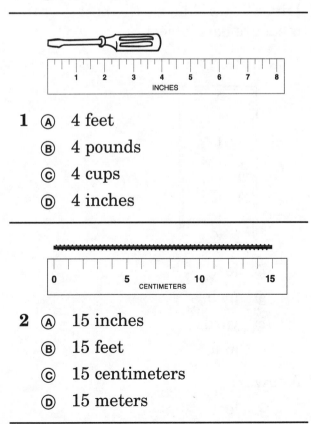

1 Ⓐ 4 feet

Ⓑ 4 pounds

Ⓒ 4 cups

Ⓓ 4 inches

2 Ⓐ 15 inches

Ⓑ 15 feet

Ⓒ 15 centimeters

Ⓓ 15 meters

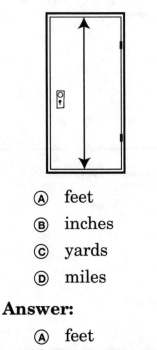

3 Ⓐ 4 ft

Ⓑ 4 in

Ⓒ 4 cm

Ⓓ 4 kg

4 Ⓐ 4 cm

Ⓑ 5 cm

Ⓒ 6 cm

Ⓓ 5 in

Directions: Choose the best way to measure each object.

Example:

Ⓐ feet

Ⓑ inches

Ⓒ yards

Ⓓ miles

Answer:

Ⓐ feet

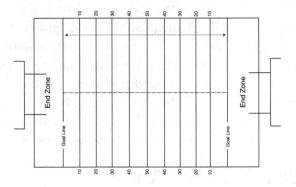

5 Ⓐ centimeters

Ⓑ inches

Ⓒ yards

Ⓓ feet

6 Ⓐ pounds

Ⓑ yards

Ⓒ miles

Ⓓ ounces

Directions: Estimate the amount shown.

7 Ⓐ about 1 cup

Ⓑ about 1 pint

Ⓒ about 1 liter

Ⓓ about 1 quart

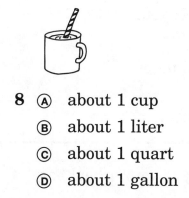

8 Ⓐ about 1 cup

Ⓑ about 1 liter

Ⓒ about 1 quart

Ⓓ about 1 gallon

Directions: Choose the correct temperature as shown on the thermometer below.

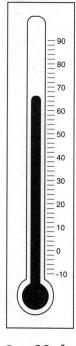

9 Ⓐ 60 degrees

Ⓑ 62 degrees

Ⓒ 66 degrees

Ⓓ 70 degrees

10 Ⓐ 40 degrees

Ⓑ 42 degrees

Ⓒ 49 degrees

Ⓓ 38 degrees

Directions: Look at the items on the scales to answer questions 11 and 12.

11 Choose the object that weighs the most.

Ⓐ book

Ⓑ bowling ball

Ⓒ cat

Ⓓ pumpkin

12 Choose the object that weighs the least.

Ⓐ book

Ⓑ bowling ball

Ⓒ cat

Ⓓ pumpkin

Directions: Choose the tool that would work best to solve the next two problems.

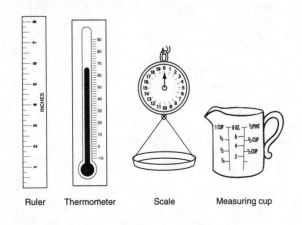

Ruler   Thermometer   Scale   Measuring cup

13 How wide is your desk?

Ⓐ ruler

Ⓑ thermometer

Ⓒ scale

Ⓓ measuring cup

14 How heavy is your school bag?

Ⓐ ruler

Ⓑ thermometer

Ⓒ scale

Ⓓ measuring cup

15 What is the area of the shape below?

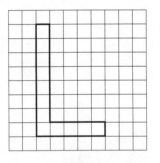

Ⓐ 16 square units

Ⓑ 14 square units

Ⓒ 10 square units

Ⓓ 12 square units

(See page 102 for answer key.)

CHAPTER 8

Geometry

Most children don't really associate geometry with math. It's too much fun and, at this level, deals very little with anything numeric—at least, this is how second graders see it. For them, it's shapes and figures, buildings and puzzles. We should try to keep it this way as we help them prepare for standardized tests. The more it seems like a game or a toy, the more successful you'll feel in your quest to help them strengthen their skills.

In second-grade geometry, children study plane (flat) shapes like circles and squares, as well as their solid (three-dimensional) counterparts, such as spheres and cubes, to name just a couple. They learn about lines and curves and symmetry and congruent shapes, and they review area and perimeter. Teachers strive to expand children's knowledge beyond "a square has four sides" and to help them to look at things in their world from all sides. As you try some geometry activities together, you may both find yourselves looking at things from a new perspective.

What Second Graders Should Know

Children in the second grade should be familiar with the four basic shapes and be able to discuss the characteristics of each (circle, square, rectangle, and triangle). Although they may not have all the terminology down pat, they should be starting to understand the concepts of parallel and perpendicular lines and be able to iden-

tify sides, edges, corners, faces, line segments, and points. Some other important vocabulary words are

sphere	*cylinder*
plane	*congruent*
square units	*octagon*
cube	*rectangular prism*
cone	*symmetrical*
hexagon	*solid*

Second graders need to show an understanding of the way shapes appear in space and from different angles. For instance, if you traced around the face of a cone, what shape would you see? (A circle.) Or if you "peel off the wrapper" of a cylinder, what shape will that be? (A rectangle.) Second graders need to be able to identify a line of symmetry, a congruent shape, and plane versus solid shapes.

What You and Your Child Can Do

Hide and Seek. Open cabinets and doors and look high and low to find objects of different shapes already hidden in your home. You may be surprised to see what you find hidden away. You might even be able to hold a geometric yard sale! Be sure to talk about what you see and the ways in which the objects resemble particular shapes.

Get a Clue. Use a few of the objects you found for the previous activity, and place them or hide them around the room. Then give clues to help your child decide which shape to retrieve. For example, "Find the solid shape that looks like a triangle at first, but its face is a circle." If your child has trouble, add more information or a hint, "You wear it on your head at a party, or eat ice cream from it." (Cone.) Another example, "Which solid shape has twelve edges and congruent faces?" (This one may take some thinking! It's a cube.) Allow your child to examine the shapes, pick them up, turn them over, etc. The more she handles them, the more familiar they will become to her.

Geoboards. These little tools are inexpensive to buy or make and are lots of fun, even if you're not studying geometry. To make one, you'll need $1/2$-inch plywood cut in a 12-inch square. Measure and mark (your second grader can help with this) 1-inch squares inside the big square so that it looks like a grid. Hammer a tiny nail at each intersection of the small squares. Then use rubber bands to make different shapes by looping them around the nails. Name a shape, and have your child form one, or make one yourself, and have her name it. If you're very ambitious, make two geoboards, and have your child replicate the shape that you make on your board, and vice versa.

Trinkets. Have your child gather some little objects with which to measure the perimeters of other objects. You'll need several of the same size trinket to make it work correctly. Paper clips, macaroni, Lego pieces, erasers, pebbles, and dried beans all work well. Then find a few things with uniform shapes, such as a book, a photograph, a CD case, a video case, or assorted cardboard boxes. Then have your child line up the trinkets around the outside edges of the shape. Count them to determine the nonstandard perimeter of each shape.

Graph Paper. This works in the same way as a geoboard, but in a less complicated way. For some reason, children love the confines of graph paper. It doesn't limit their creativity; it just channels it in a new direction. Allow your second grader to create scenes by tracing the lines on the paper to make objects, real or imagined. Then go back and talk about her picture. Choose an object, and ask her to find the perimeter of it by counting the unit lines around the outside. She also can find the area by counting the square units inside the object.

Parquetry Tiles. These neat little do-dads have been around for a long time. You may have even played with them yourself as a child. Parquetry tiles are flat wooden shapes painted with basic colors. They can be arranged in a zillion different ways to make different designs and objects, kind of like stained glass windows. Sometimes they come with patterns to reproduce or pictures to create. They help children to see the relationships between shapes and the way they fit (or don't fit) together. You can buy them at educational toy stores, and sometimes you can find them in the puzzle section of a department store.

What Tests May Ask

Most standardized tests don't ask very many obvious geometry questions. Instead, items involving geometry may appear as applied mathematics questions. There will be a few questions that ask children to look at geometric shapes in a certain sequence and then complete or continue the pattern. Other questions may ask a child to identify a shape by its name or to find a real-world object with a comparable shape. For instance, a basketball is a sphere, and a can of soda is a cylinder. A test also most likely will ask students to identify a line of symmetry, congruent shapes, and open and closed shapes and to measure area and perimeter of given shapes using standard or nonstandard units.

Practice Skill: Geometry

Directions: Read each question below, and choose the correct figure.

Example: Choose the rectangular prism.

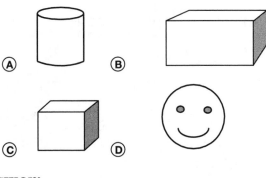

Answer:

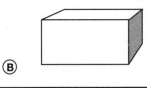

Ⓑ

---

1 Which picture is a cylinder?

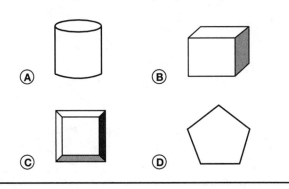

---

2 Choose the shape without sides.

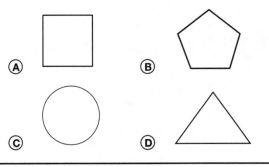

3 Which two shapes put together would make a rectangle?

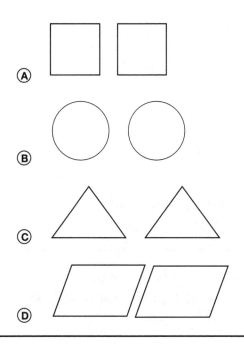

---

4 Choose the shape that will complete the pattern shown below.

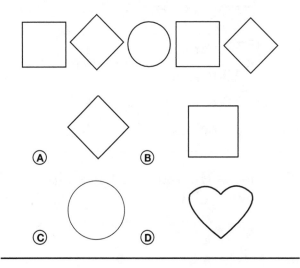

---

5 Look at the picture. How many units are shown in the rectangle?

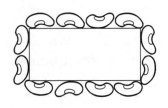

- Ⓐ 12 units
- Ⓑ 22 units
- Ⓒ 10 square units
- Ⓓ 8 square units

6 How many beans would fit around the perimenter of this shape?

- Ⓐ 8 beans
- Ⓑ 10 beans
- Ⓒ 12 beans
- Ⓓ 14 beans

7 Choose the name of the shape shown below.

STOP

- Ⓐ hexagon
- Ⓑ octagon
- Ⓒ pentagon
- Ⓓ decagon

8 How many triangles do you see in the picture below?

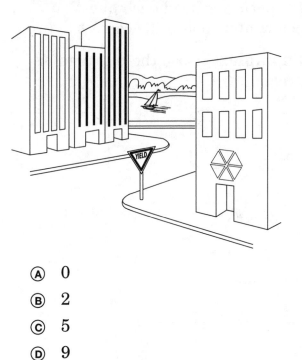

- Ⓐ 0
- Ⓑ 2
- Ⓒ 5
- Ⓓ 9

9 Choose the one figure below that is *not* a triangle.

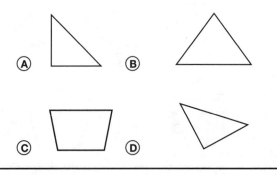

(See page 102 for answer key.)

CHAPTER 9

Fractions

Most traditional math textbooks immediately follow a unit on geometry with a unit on fractions. Sometimes they are combined into one area of study because in many ways they go hand in hand.

Geometry presents shapes—and then the study of fractions teaches ways to break those same shapes into smaller equal pieces. Learning about fractions combines many skills that children learn throughout second grade, so it often appears about halfway through the year. It is also the perfect (albeit often missed) opportunity for children to build the foundation for their understanding of numbers less than one, or parts of a whole.

We don't have to use the word *decimal,* but this concept is one that is generally kept for higher grades when it could be aptly taught in second grade.

What Second Graders Should Know

By the time they begin second grade, most children have not had too much exposure to fractions in a classroom setting. A page or two in first grade sets the groundwork, but the subject hasn't been formally taught until now. However, children have a storehouse of real-life experiences that will be invaluable in their understanding of fractions.

Did your child ever eat pizza? How about a sandwich? Has he baked brownies? Has he folded a sheet of paper? These skills are all built on when learning about fractions.

The first thing second graders are taught about fractions is to look at shapes to determine whether or not they are divided into equal parts. The number of parts is less important at this point, but the key is to see the parts of the whole shape.

The next step is to name the parts of a fraction. Although it most likely will *not* appear on a test, students may hear the terms *numerator* and *denominator.* Just to refresh your memory, the denominator is the bottom numeral. (Remember: *d*enominator = *d*own; on the bottom.) The denominator represents the whole shape or the number of parts into which the whole shape has been "cut." The numerator is the top numeral. It "numbers" the pieces of the whole or tells how many parts of the whole we're dealing with at the moment. Thus, in the fraction

$$^3/_4$$

which can be represented by shading three or four equal-sized squares in the box below:

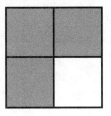

$\dfrac{3}{4}$ is the number of shaded parts (numerator).

4 is the total number of parts (denominator).

Fractions in the second grade are kept pretty simple and almost always should be shown in picture form first. Remember, at this level children learn best when they can see or touch something concrete. Once this is mastered, they can learn in a more abstract way.

Your second grader is ready to work with halves, thirds, fourths, fifths, sixths, eighths, and tenths. He also may be ready to show how some fractions are equal, even though the numerals in each may differ.

Finally, second graders should notice that objects in groups often represent fractions and can be treated as such. In the example below, there are five hearts, and three of them are shaded. Several fractions could represent these pictures.

What fraction of the hearts are shaded? ($^{3}/_{5}$)

What fraction of the hearts are white? ($^{2}/_{5}$)

What fraction represents all the hearts? ($^{5}/_{5}$)

What fraction represents none of the hearts? ($^{0}/_{5}$)

What You and Your Child Can Do

Origami, Anyone? This paper folding isn't nearly as complicated as one might think, and it helps children see how the relationships between fractions unfold (literally). Begin with any piece of paper, one from school is fine (reduce, reuse, recycle!). Fold it in half, and then open it. In any chosen color, have your child write ½ in each space. Then refold the paper, and fold it again. This time when it's opened, write ¼ in each of the four spaces in a different color. Continue folding and labeling the parts of the whole until you can't fold the paper anymore. Open it up, and look for equivalent fractions or other patterns you might find. Ask your child to name the different fractions.

Paper Plate Pies. You'll need to prepare this activity a bit in advance, but your child certainly can help. Cut paper plates into equal "pie pieces" to represent halves, thirds, fourths, fifths, sixths, eighths, and tenths. Have your child color or paint the pieces, using a different color for each plate. He also can label each piece ½, ⅓, ¼, etc. Then mix the pieces, and ask her to put the plates back together like puzzles. Compare pieces to determine equivalent fractions and to show that fractions with a greater number in the denominator are actually smaller than fractions with lesser denominators. For example, even though 8 is greater than 2, ⅛ is less than ½.

Be a Hero. A hero sandwich, that is! Using the same ideas as the paper plate pies, assemble paper sandwiches with your child. Have him cut them into equal portions (these will vary depending on the shape of the "bread" that he chooses). Of course, you can use real sandwiches, too! If you use square bread, ask your child to find out how many ways he knows to cut the bread into fourths or quarters. You may be surprised at his creativity!

Don't Forget Your Change. The direct link between money and fractions is invaluable when teaching both concepts, so save your pocket change! You'll need enough of each coin to equal $1 and a one dollar bill. Begin with two half dollars (50-cent pieces). Using tape or small stickers, label the coins with the appropriate fractions. Talk about how many half dollars it takes to equal one dollar and why the name of the coin is a *half dollar.* Be patient. Many of the things that are obvious to us seem that way because someone took the time to teach us. Next, go to the quarter. Spread out four of them, and label each one ¼. Talk about how many quarters equal one dollar. See if your child knows other things that are measured in quarters, such as four quarter hours on a clock, four grading quarters in an academic year, and the four quarts in a gallon. Continue the pattern and the discussion with dimes, nickels, and pennies. Do yourself a favor, and don't label all the pennies! It's pretty exciting for children to grasp the concept of 1/100, and the fact that it's the *smallest* piece of a whole that they've ever heard of is just plain cool!

Measure Up? Back to the sand, water, or rice bucket! Using liquid and dry measuring cups and measuring spoons, put your child to "work" determining how many of each smaller cup it takes to fill the one-cup container. Be sure to ask your child *why* things work out the way they do, and encourage him to write the reason in sentence form.

What Tests May Ask

Several questions on a standardized test will pertain to fractions. Most of these will ask students to identify a picture showing a given fraction, or just the opposite: Students will be asked to choose a fraction to match a picture. There will be one or two items that ask students to identify equal parts, and possibly a few items showing fractions represented by objects in groups.

On many newer tests, children will find a written component that will ask for an answer as well as a sentence or two that explains the student's reasoning or thought processes. This is a skill that may require more practice than any

other, so ask your child what made him choose an answer or complete a question in a certain way. Have him write it in a sentence and read it back to you as well.

Practice Skill: Fractions

Directions: Read each question below, and choose the correct answer.

Example:

Choose the shape that shows equal parts.

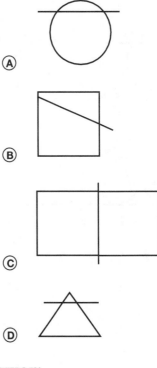

Answer:

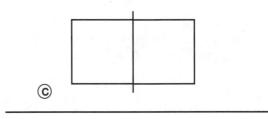

1 Choose the shape that shows equal parts.

2 Choose the shape that does not have equal parts.

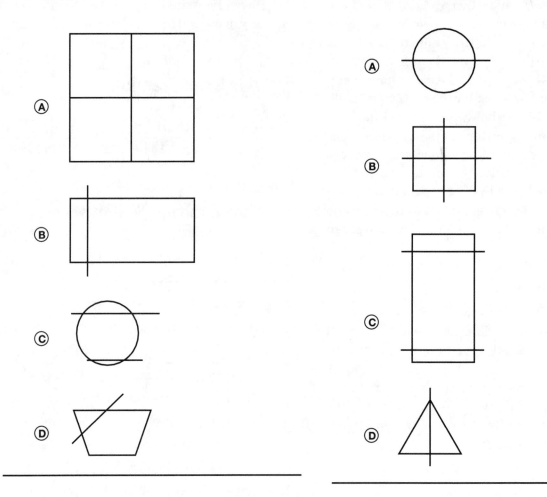

Directions: Choose the fraction that is the same as the shaded part of each shape.

Example:

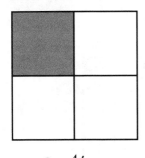

   Ⓐ 4/4

   Ⓑ 4/1

   Ⓒ 1/4

   Ⓓ 1/1

Answer:

   Ⓒ 1/4

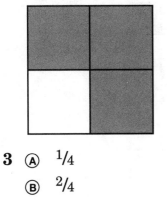

3 Ⓐ 1/4

    Ⓑ 2/4

    Ⓒ 3/4

    Ⓓ 4/4

4 Ⓐ 3/8

    Ⓑ 3/5

    Ⓒ 5/3

    Ⓓ 5/8

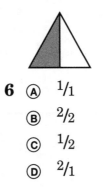

5 Ⓐ 1/5

    Ⓑ 2/5

    Ⓒ 5/2

    Ⓓ 2/3

6 Ⓐ 1/1

    Ⓑ 2/2

    Ⓒ 1/2

    Ⓓ 2/1

Directions: Choose the picture that means the same thing as the fraction.

Example:

1/6

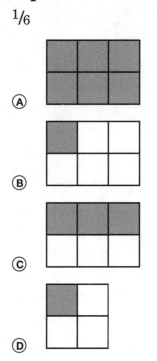

Answer:

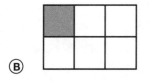

7 3/4

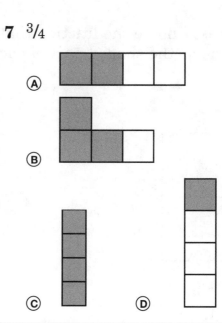

8 2/3

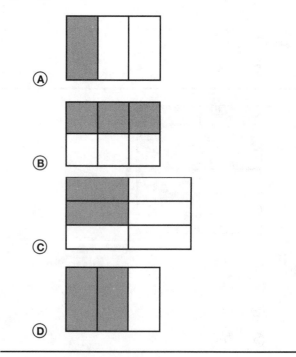

9 $^2/_2$

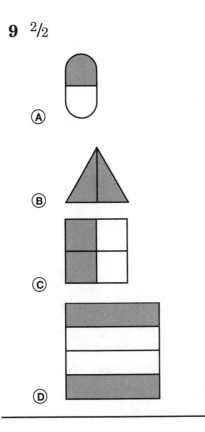

Ⓐ

Ⓑ

Ⓒ

Ⓓ

10 In the fraction $^2/_6$, how many equal parts are there?

Ⓐ 2

Ⓑ 8

Ⓒ 6

Ⓓ 4

11 What fraction of the marbles below are gray?

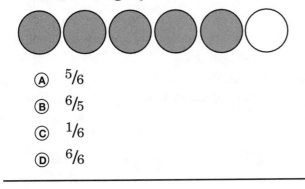

Ⓐ $^5/_6$

Ⓑ $^6/_5$

Ⓒ $^1/_6$

Ⓓ $^6/_6$

12 What fraction of the birds pictured below are flying?

Ⓐ $^2/_3$

Ⓑ $^3/_2$

Ⓒ $^5/_3$

Ⓓ $^3/_5$

13 What fraction of the trees pictured below have leaves?

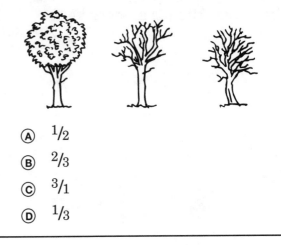

Ⓐ $^1/_2$

Ⓑ $^2/_3$

Ⓒ $^3/_1$

Ⓓ $^1/_3$

14 Which shape shows the same as ⅓?

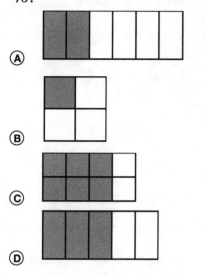

Ⓐ

Ⓑ

Ⓒ

Ⓓ

(See page 102 for answer key.)

CHAPTER 10

Multiplication and More

Wow! We've covered a lot of territory in just a few pages, but we're not finished yet. Every standardized test has several one-item skills sandwiched inside. These concepts are usually those which are taught briefly during a given school year as review or those which are newly introduced and are not fully developed in the curriculum for a particular grade level. The list may be different depending on the geographic area in which you live.

Some school districts, counties, and states may mandate the curriculum to include these skills as core mastery skills, whereas others may not. It all depends on your child's school. In second grade, the skills most likely to be treated as supplemental are multiplication, division, probability, rounding, and the data analysis that accompanies graphs, tables, and charts. Don't panic if your child seems a little bewildered at the mention of these ideas. There are schools where these concepts are taught only in third grade or beyond. In fact, this is one of the things the tests determine; standardized tests assess not only the individual child but also children as groups within a district, county, or state.

It's up to you to decide whether or not to tackle these new areas if they are unfamiliar to your child. Included in this chapter are simple ways to introduce and practice these ideas, but it's your choice. Remember that some children will pick up on new concepts very quickly, thinking they're fun or exciting. For others, the pressure of learning these skills in "crash course" fashion is very disconcerting. Of course, you know your child best and can make this determination.

What Second Graders Should Know

By the end of the year, most second graders will be exposed to multiplication in one way or another. Some will have direct instruction, and others may encounter it during computer-assisted practice sessions or in the form of an enrichment activity. Most students should recognize that multiplication is the combining of groups of objects. Exercises in skip-counting (counting by 2s, 3s, 5s, and 10s), repeated addition, and counting objects in groups are all part of the process. Some children will be able to look at a picture of objects in groups, construct a simple multiplication problem, and then solve it. Some may see a multiplication math sentence ($3 \times 4 =$ ___) and know exactly what to do, whereas others may not have the faintest idea where to begin.

The same scenario holds for division. Some children will have discovered by one source or another that division involves putting objects into equal groupings. They may not know all the vocabulary or understand the concept completely, but the basic idea should strike a familiar chord with about half of ending second graders.

The word *probability* might not roll off your child's tongue with certainty, but she probably has played a game involving it or has figured out some of the components by herself. She should recognize the way odds increase or decrease depending on certain factors, but instead of the word *odds,* she may know that something is "very likely" to occur or "probably" will happen.

Rounding also may be presented on a standardized test, but it usually isn't taught to second graders as such. At this level, students generally are asked to "find the nearest ten." Given a number between 1 and 100, most second graders should be able to find the closest ten by looking at a number line. They also may be able to figure this out without a visual aid.

Early in their elementary school careers, children begin learning about data analysis, but they wouldn't know it if you asked them! Primary school teachers construct basic pictographs to show information that is meaningful to their young students. In the hallways of many elementary schools you'll find graphs depicting students' favorite ice cream flavors, favorite colors, number of siblings, or kinds of pets. Second graders should be able to identify a pictograph (where a picture symbol represents one or sometimes more than one), read the *title* of the graph, locate and comprehend the *key,* and interpret the *data* (they'll call it information) found within. They also should be able to reverse the process, looking at information and constructing a graph to depict what they see. Students should be able to do the same for a bar graph, a simple chart, and a table (most familiar are the table of contents at the beginning of a book and an addition table).

What You and Your Child Can Do

Multiplication Made Easy. The best way to teach multiplication (and many other math concepts) begins with manipulatives—dried beans, pennies, buttons, bingo chips, and so on. Let your child practice putting them into equal groups and then counting the total of all the beans in all the groups. The words *groups of* are a crucial part of understanding the process of multiplication. Children need to see that they are actually adding groups of objects and repeating that addition as many times as the problem directs. As your child writes a multiplication "sentence" or problem, teach her to say out loud "groups of" as she draws the strokes of the multiplication symbol. For example, as she writes the sentence $3 \times 4 = 12$, she should say "3 groups of 4 = 12" and write each stroke of the $\times$ with each word. This little habit will help her to understand the process as well as eliminate confusion between problems.

2 by 4s. Even though a trip to the hardware store would be fun and educational, using graph paper and crayons or markers is a bit more practical. Talk to your child about the meanings of the lumber measurements 2×4, 2×6, and 4×8 plywood. You could even build a birdhouse or a toy box for the garage if you're really ambitious. For our purposes, however, using graph paper to make boxes of various sizes will work. Guide your child to make several different boxes, and note the number of grid squares going up one side and across the bottom. Then ask her to figure out the total number of grid squares without counting them.

Opportunity Knocks. Keep your eyes open for opportunities to multiply. There are lots of them, but you don't want to overwhelm your child. Look for the patterns that show a number of objects across and a number down, such as a muffin tin (3×4 or 2×3), panes in a window, or an egg carton. When you feel that your child understands these examples, move to a more imaginative approach, calculating the total number of fingers on your whole family's hands, the number of legs on all the neighborhood dogs, the number of wheels on the bikes of all your friends, etc.

Share and Share Alike. Using the manipulative counters mentioned earlier, begin with an easily divided number of them and use your imagination! Ask your child to pretend that she has 15 cookies and has to share them with her two friends. What would the division problem be? Fifteen divided by three equals what ($15 \div 3 =$ ___)? Use real cookies and real paper plates for even more fun! The first number in the problem represents the number of cookies, and the second number represents the number of plates or friends. Be sure your second grader writes the division sentence that goes with each problem that she solves.

What Are the Chances? This simple game of probability is neat for kids and adults. Get a small paper bag or other opaque container. Get about 25 pennies and 5 dimes (or other manipulatives that are different colors, such as marbles, checkers, or popsicle sticks). Whatever you choose, use about 20 that are alike and 3 to 5 with a different characteristic (color the tips of four of the craft sticks red and one blue). First, put one object of each color in the bag. Predict the chances that each color will be chosen when all three are in the bag, then test your theory by pulling out one stick at a time, ten times. Keep track of the results by tally, or ask your child to color a dot or a little square for each try. For the next round, add the rest of the red objects into the mix, and discuss how the odds have changed. Now that you have one plain, one blue, and four red, objects, which color is likely to appear most often? Which color is least likely to be chosen?

Super Spinners. For this probability activity, you'll need a few small paper plates, crayons or markers, a sharp pencil, and a paper clip. Help your child to divide each plate into five different sized "pie slices." Your child can color or number each slice. Examine the sizes of the slices, and talk about which slice takes up the most and which takes up the least space. Place the paper clip on the plate, and put the point of the pencil through one end in the middle of the plate. This becomes the spinner. Give it a few test flicks to be sure it works well, and then make your predictions. Based on the sizes of the slices, if you were to spin ten times, how many times do you think each slice will be chosen? Is it likely or not likely that the smallest slice will be chosen?

How likely is it that the largest slice will be chosen? On a piece of paper, note your predictions. Then start spinning! At the end of ten spins, whose predictions were more accurate? Look at another plate with slices of different sizes. Make new predictions, and always talk about why things turned out the way they did.

Jump Around! Remember that giant number line that you drew on the sidewalk a few chapters back? It will work perfectly for this rounding activity, but if it's raining, you'll have to go to plan B. Use a really long piece of masking tape in a hallway or other long indoor space. If you really want to "do it up right," mark a number every 2 inches or so, from 0 to 100. Give your child a randomly chosen number, out of a hat or out of thin air, and have her stand near it. Ask her to jump, or round, to the nearest ten. Many second graders haven't been taught the term *round* as a verb, so "find the nearest ten" is equally acceptable. After she's practiced this a few times, shake things up a bit by asking your child to add or subtract rounded numbers. For example, "$39 + 28$ is about ___." Talk through the process together. "Thirty-nine is about 40 and 28 is about 30, so the sum would be about 70." Also have your child move to the appropriate spots on the number line to put the process into action.

Sports Page. Ask your child to sit down with you and read the sports page of the newspaper. After all the postgame articles and event summaries, there are usually a bunch of little tables showing team statistics and other information. Help your child to see the meaning of the different number patterns and data shown on the various tables. Choose a sport and a team to follow throughout the season, and clip the tables and charts to compare from week to week.

Be on the Lookout. As you read through newspapers, magazines, and other sources of literature, clip or at least dog-ear samples of any kind of graph. Talk about the reason for the graph (what it's really showing) and the meaning of symbols. Ask questions about it that a child can understand and answer. "Which company sold the most soda last year?" "What does this short bar tell us about the number of elephants in Kenya?" Being able to read and interpret the graph is the most important part, so if you find a graph that really isn't suitable for a second-grade mind, skip it and look for a better one.

Make It Yourself. If you have a computer, you can work with your child to create your own charts, graphs, and tables with the touch of a button. Think of some easily accessed information that you could use, and make it interesting for your second grader (your company's sales figures from last month don't count!). Maybe you could keep track of how many times in a month your family eats out or how many people in your extended family have birthdays in certain months. Click on that "Create a Table" icon, and away you go. Your child most likely will surprise you with the ideas she has for other things you can graph together.

What Tests May Ask

As mentioned earlier, standardized tests don't devote very much space to the aforementioned concepts, probably a question or two on each. However, a recent emphasis on state standards and thinking skills has led to changes in the format of some tests. They may include a written component that asks children to explain how they arrived at an answer or why their response makes sense to them. This most likely will show up with the graphing questions but possibly could appear anywhere with any concept.

Students at this grade can anticipate finding basic multiplication and division problems on standardized tests. They also may be asked to draw a picture of the problem or choose a problem that matches a picture. Rounding to the

nearest ten and probability items may or may not be included, but there definitely will be a graph, table, or chart to interpret, followed by several questions relating to it.

Second graders should expect to see some things that they just don't understand because they've never seen them before. There won't be very many of them, but you can help by preparing your child for the inevitable. If you calmly explain that there will be parts of the test that may be a little tricky, hopefully she will take the same approach. She should look at each question carefully and think about what the possible answer could be. Making an educated guess is better than leaving it blank, and worrying or getting upset won't do any good.

Practice Skill: Multiplication and More

Directions: Choose the multiplication problem that best matches the picture.

Example:

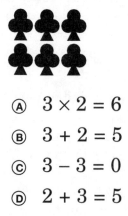

 Ⓐ $3 \times 2 = 6$

 Ⓑ $3 + 2 = 5$

 Ⓒ $3 - 3 = 0$

 Ⓓ $2 + 3 = 5$

Answer:

 Ⓐ $3 \times 2 = 6$

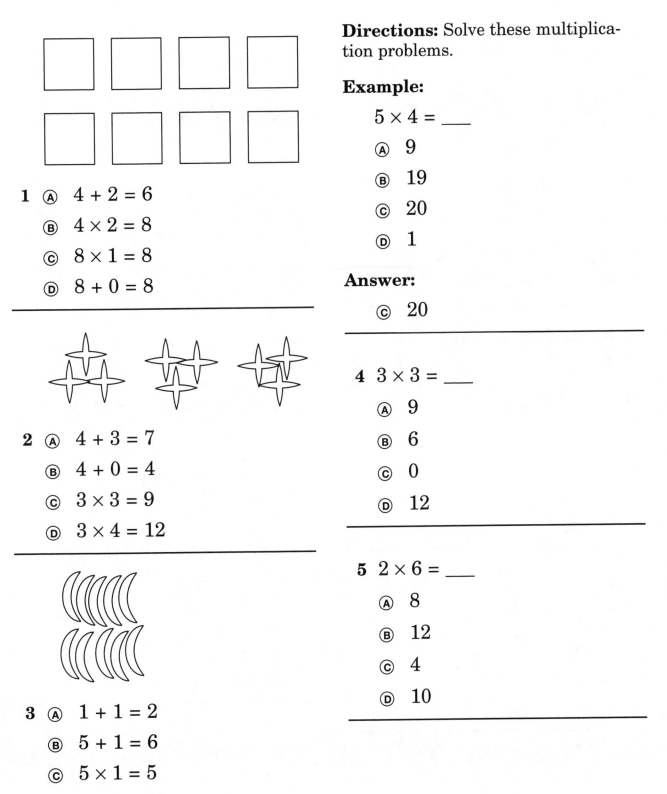

1 (A) $4 + 2 = 6$

(B) $4 \times 2 = 8$

(C) $8 \times 1 = 8$

(D) $8 + 0 = 8$

2 (A) $4 + 3 = 7$

(B) $4 + 0 = 4$

(C) $3 \times 3 = 9$

(D) $3 \times 4 = 12$

3 (A) $1 + 1 = 2$

(B) $5 + 1 = 6$

(C) $5 \times 1 = 5$

(D) $2 \times 5 = 10$

Directions: Solve these multiplication problems.

Example:

$5 \times 4 = \underline{}$

(A) 9

(B) 19

(C) 20

(D) 1

Answer:

(C) 20

4 $3 \times 3 = \underline{}$

(A) 9

(B) 6

(C) 0

(D) 12

5 $2 \times 6 = \underline{}$

(A) 8

(B) 12

(C) 4

(D) 10

Directions: Choose the division problem that matches the picture.

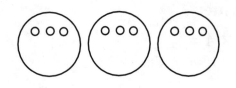

6 Ⓐ 3 + 3 = 6

Ⓑ 3 ÷ 3 = 1

Ⓒ 6 ÷ 3 = 2

Ⓓ 9 ÷ 3 = 3

Directions: Solve these division problems.

7 15 ÷ 5 = ___

Ⓐ 20

Ⓑ 10

Ⓒ 3

Ⓓ 45

8 6 ÷ 2 = ___

Ⓐ 8

Ⓑ 4

Ⓒ 3

Ⓓ 2

9 What is 58 to the nearest ten?

Ⓐ 50

Ⓑ 60

Ⓒ 55

Ⓓ 65

Directions: Look at the graph below carefully. Use this graph to answer questions 10 through 12.

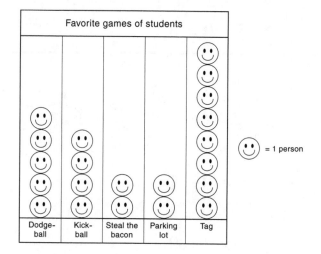

10 The graph tells the class's favorite

_____.

Ⓐ color

Ⓑ song

Ⓒ game

Ⓓ food

11 Which game is the favorite of the most children?

Ⓐ kickball

Ⓑ tag

Ⓒ dodgeball

Ⓓ parking lot

12 How many more children like dodgeball than parking lot?

Ⓐ 6

Ⓑ 5

Ⓒ 4

Ⓓ 3

(See page 102 for answer key.)

Web Sites and Resources for More Information

Homework

Homework Central
http://www.HomeworkCentral.com
Terrific site for students, parents, and teachers, filled with information, projects, and more.

Win the Homework Wars
(Sylvan Learning Centers)
http://www.educate.com/online/qa_peters.html

Reading and Grammar Help

Born to Read: How to Raise a Reader
http://www.ala.org/alsc/raise_a_reader.html

Guide to Grammar and Writing
http://webster.commnet.edu/hp/pages/darling/grammar.htm
Help with "plague words and phrases," grammar FAQs, sentence parts, punctuation, rules for common usage.

Internet Public Library: Reading Zone
http://www.ipl.org/cgi-bin/youth/youth.out

Keeping Kids Reading and Writing
http://www.tiac.net/users/maryl/

U.S. Dept. of Education: Helping Your Child Learn to Read
http://www.ed.gov/pubs/parents/Reading/index.html

Math Help

Center for Advancement of Learning
http://www.muskingum.edu/%7Ecal/database/Math2.html
Substitution and memory strategies for math.

Center for Advancement of Learning
http://www.muskingum.edu/%7Ecal/database/Math1.html
General tips and suggestions.

Math.com
http://www.math.com
The world of math online.

Math.com
http://www.math.com/student/testprep.html
Get ready for standardized tests.

Math.com: Homework Help in Math
http://www.math.com/students/homework.html

Math.com: Math for Homeschoolers
http://www.math.com/parents/homeschool.html

The Math Forum: Problems and Puzzles
http://forum.swarthmore.edu/library/resource_types/problems_puzzles
Lots of fun math puzzles and problems for grades K through 12.

The Math Forum: Math Tips and Tricks
http://forum.swarthmore.edu/k12/mathtips/mathtips.html

Tips on Testing

Books on Test Preparation
http://www.testbooksonline.com/preHS.asp
This site provides printed resources for parents who wish to help their children prepare for standardized school tests.

Core Knowledge Web Site
http://www.coreknowledge.org/
Site dedicated to providing resources for parents; based on the books of E. D. Hirsch, Jr., who wrote the *What Your X Grader Needs to Know* series.

Family Education Network
http://www.familyeducation.com/article/0,1120,1-6219,00.html
This report presents some of the arguments against current standardized testing practices in the public schools. The site also provides links to family activities that help kids learn.

Math.com
http://www.math.com/students/testprep.html
Get ready for standardized tests.

Standardized Tests
http://arc.missouri.edu/k12/
K through 12 assessment tools and know-how.

Parents: Testing in Schools

KidSource: Talking to Your Child's Teacher about Standardized Tests
http://www.kidsource.com/kidsource/content2/talking.assessment.k12.4.html
This site provides basic information to help parents understand their children's test results and provides pointers for how to discuss the results with their children's teachers.

eSCORE.com: State Test and Education Standards
http://www.eSCORE.com
Find out if your child meets the necessary requirements for your local schools. A Web site with experts from Brazelton Institute and Harvard's Project Zero.

Overview of States' Assessment Programs
http://ericae.net/faqs/

Parent Soup
Education Central: Standardized Tests
http://www.parentsoup.com/edcentral/testing
A parent's guide to standardized testing in the schools, written from a parent advocacy standpoint.

National Center for Fair and Open Testing, Inc. (FairTest)
342 Broadway
Cambridge, MA 02139
(617) 864-4810
http://www.fairtest.org

National Parent Information Network
http://npin.org

Publications for Parents from the U.S. Department of Education
http://www.ed.gov/pubs/parents/
An ever-changing list of information for parents available from the U.S. Department of Education.

State of the States Report
http://www.edweek.org/sreports/qc99/states/indicators/in-intro.htm
A report on testing and achievement in the 50 states.

Testing: General Information

Academic Center for Excellence
http://www.acekids.com

American Association for Higher Education Assessment
http://www.aahe.org/assessment/web.htm

American Educational Research Association (AERA)
http://aera.net
An excellent link to reports on American education, including reports on the controversy over standardized testing.

American Federation of Teachers
555 New Jersey Avenue, NW
Washington, D.C. 20011

Association of Test Publishers Member Products and Services

http://www.testpublishers.org/memserv.htm

Education Week on the Web

http://www.edweek.org

ERIC Clearinghouse on Assessment and Evaluation

1131 Shriver Lab
University of Maryland
College Park, MD 20742

http://ericae.net

A clearinghouse of information on assessment and education reform.

FairTest: The National Center for Fair and Open Testing

http://fairtest.org/facts/ntfact.htm
http://fairtest.org/

The National Center for Fair and Open Testing is an advocacy organization working to end the abuses, misuses, and flaws of standardized testing and to ensure that evaluation of students and workers is fair, open, and educationally sound. This site provides many links to fact sheets, opinion papers, and other sources of information about testing.

National Congress of Parents and Teachers

700 North Rush Street
Chicago, Illinois 60611

National Education Association

1201 16th Street, NW
Washington, DC 20036

National School Boards Association

http://www.nsba.org

A good source for information on all aspects of public education, including standardized testing.

Testing Our Children: A Report Card on State Assessment Systems

http://www.fairtest.org/states/survey.htm
Report of testing practices of the states, with graphical links to the states and a critique of fair testing practices in each state.

Trends in Statewide Student Assessment Programs: A Graphical Summary

http://www.ccsso.org/survey96.html
Results of annual survey of states' departments of public instruction regarding their testing practices.

U.S. Department of Education

http://www.ed.gov/

Web Links for Parents Who Want to Help Their Children Achieve

http://www.liveandlearn.com/learn.html
This page offers many Web links to free and for-sale information and materials for parents who want to help their children do well in school. Titles include such free offerings as the Online Colors Game and questionnaires to determine whether your child is ready for school.

What Should Parents Know about Standardized Testing in the Schools?

http://www.rusd.k12.ca.us/parents/standard.html
An online brochure about standardized testing in the schools, with advice regarding how to become an effective advocate for your child.

Test Publishers Online

ACT: Information for Life's Transitions

http://www.act.org

American Guidance Service, Inc.

http://www.agsnet.com

Ballard & Tighe Publishers

http://www.ballard-tighe.com

Consulting Psychologists Press

http://www.cpp-db.com

CTB McGraw-Hill

http://www.ctb.com

Educational Records Bureau

http://www.erbtest.org/index.html

Educational Testing Service

http://www.ets.org

General Educational Development (GED) Testing Service
http://www.acenet.edu/calec/ged/home.html

Harcourt Brace Educational Measurement
http://www.hbem.com

Piney Mountain Press—A Cyber-Center for Career and Applied Learning
http://www.pineymountain.com

ProEd Publishing
http://www.proedinc.com

Riverside Publishing Company
http://www.hmco.com/hmco/riverside

Stoelting Co.
http://www.stoeltingco.com

Sylvan Learning Systems, Inc.
http://www.educate.com

Touchstone Applied Science Associates, Inc. (TASA)
http://www.tasa.com

Tests Online

(*Note:* We don't endorse tests; some may not have technical documentation. Evaluate the quality of any testing program before making decisions based on its use.)

Edutest, Inc.
http://www.edutest.com
Edutest is an Internet-accessible testing service that offers criterion-referenced tests for elementary school students, based upon the standards for K through 12 learning and achievement in the states of Virginia, California, and Florida.

Virtual Knowledge
http://www.smarterkids.com
This commercial service, which enjoys a formal partnership with Sylvan Learning Centers, offers a line of skills assessments for preschool through grade 9 for use in the classroom or the home. For free online sample tests, see the Virtual Test Center.

Read More about It

Abbamont, Gary W. *Test Smart: Ready-to-Use Test-Taking Strategies and Activities for Grades 5–12.* Upper Saddle River, NJ: Prentice Hall Direct, 1997.

Cookson, Peter W., and Joshua Halberstam. *A Parent's Guide to Standardized Tests in School: How to Improve Your Child's Chances for Success.* New York: Learning Express, 1998.

Frank, Steven, and Stephen Frank. *Test-Taking Secrets: Study Better, Test Smarter, and Get Great Grades (The Backpack Study Series).* Holbrook, MA: Adams Media Corporation, 1998.

Gilbert, Sara Dulaney. *How to Do Your Best on Tests: A Survival Guide.* New York: Beech Tree Books, 1998.

Gruber, Gary. *Dr. Gary Gruber's Essential Guide to Test-Taking for Kids, Grades 3–5.* New York: William Morrow & Co., 1986.

———. *Gary Gruber's Essential Guide to Test-Taking for Kids, Grades 6, 7, 8, 9.* New York: William Morrow & Co., 1997.

Leonhardt, Mary. *99 Ways to Get Kids to Love Reading and 100 Books They'll Love.* New York: Crown, 1997.

———. *Parents Who Love Reading, Kids Who Don't: How It Happens and What You Can Do about It.* New York: Crown, 1995.

McGrath, Barbara B. *The Baseball Counting Book.* Watertown, MA: Charlesbridge, 1999.

———. *More M&M's Brand Chocolate Candies Math.* Watertown, MA: Charlesbridge, 1998.

Mokros, Janice R. *Beyond Facts & Flashcards: Exploring Math with Your Kids.* Portsmouth, NH: Heinemann, 1996.

Romain, Trevor, and Elizabeth Verdick. *True or False?: Tests Stink!* Minneapolis: Free Spirit Publishing Co., 1999.

Schartz, Eugene M. *How to Double Your Child's Grades in School: Build Brilliance and Leadership into Your Child—from Kindergarten to College—in Just 5 Minutes a Day.* New York: Barnes & Noble, 1999.

Taylor, Kathe, and Sherry Walton. *Children at the Center: A Workshop Approach to Standardized Test Preparation, K–8.* Portsmouth, NH: Heinemann, 1998.

Tobia, Sheila. *Overcoming Math Anxiety.* New York: W. W. Norton & Company, Inc., 1995.

Tufariello, Ann Hunt. *Up Your Grades: Proven Strategies for Academic Success.* Lincolnwood, IL: VGM Career Horizons, 1996.

Vorderman, Carol. *How Math Works.* Pleasantville, NY: Reader's Digest Association, Inc., 1996.

Zahler, Kathy A. *50 Simple Things You Can Do to Raise a Child Who Loves to Read.* New York: IDG Books, 1997.

What Your Child's Test Scores Mean

Several weeks or months after your child has taken standardized tests, you will receive a report such as the TerraNova Home Report found in Figures 1 and 2. You will receive similar reports if your child has taken other tests. We briefly examine what information the reports include.

Look at the first page of the Home Report. Note that the chart provides labeled bars showing the child's performance. Each bar is labeled with the child's National Percentile for that skill area. When you know how to interpret them, national percentiles can be the most useful scores you encounter on reports such as this. Even when you are confronted with different tests that use different scale scores, you can always interpret percentiles the same way, regardless of the test. A percentile tells the percent of students who score at or below that level. A percentile of 25, for example, means that 25 percent of children taking the test scored at or below that score. (It also means that 75 percent of students scored above that score.) Note that the average is always at the 50th percentile.

On the right side of the graph on the first page of the report, the publisher has designated the ranges of scores that constitute average, above average, and below average. You can also use this slightly more precise key for interpreting percentiles:

PERCENTILE RANGE	LEVEL
2 and Below	Deficient
3–8	Borderline
9–23	Low Average
24–75	Average
76–97	High Average
98 and Up	Superior

The second page of the Home report provides a listing of the child's strengths and weaknesses, along with keys for mastery, partial mastery, and non-mastery of the skills. Scoring services determine these breakdowns based on the child's scores as compared with those from the national norm group.

Your child's teacher or guidance counselor will probably also receive a profile report similar to the TerraNova Individual Profile Report, shown in Figures 3 and 4. That report will be kept in your child's permanent record. The first aspect of this report to notice is that the scores are expressed both numerically and graphically.

First look at the score bands under National Percentile. Note that the scores are expressed as bands, with the actual score represented by a dot within each band. The reason we express the scores as bands is to provide an idea of the amount by which typical scores may vary for each student. That is, each band represents a

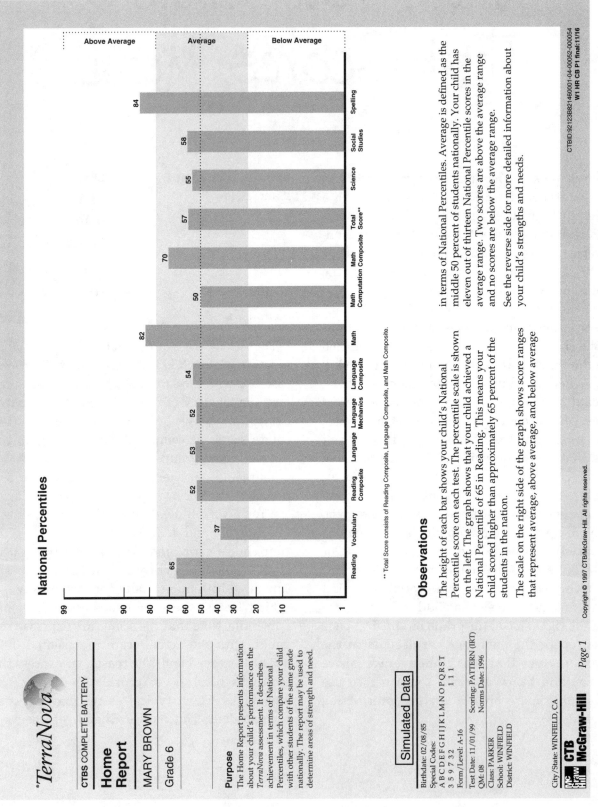

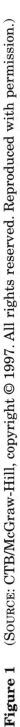

Figure 1 (SOURCE: CTB/McGraw-Hill, copyright © 1997. All rights reserved. Reproduced with permission.)

Strengths

Reading
- ● Basic Understanding
- ● Analyze Text

Vocabulary
- ● Word Meaning
- ● Words in Context

Language
- ● Editing Skills
- ● Sentence Structure

Language Mechanics
- ● Sentences, Phrases, Clauses

Mathematics
- ● Computation and Numerical Estimation
- ● Operation Concepts

Mathematics Computation
- ● Add Whole Numbers
- ● Multiply Whole Numbers

Science
- ● Life Science
- ● Inquiry Skills

Social Studies
- ● Geographic Perspectives
- ● Economic Perspectives

Spelling
- ● Vowels
- ● Consonants

Key ● Mastery

General Interpretation

The left column shows your child's best areas of performance. In each case, your child has reached mastery level. The column at the right shows the areas within each test section where your child's scores are the lowest. In these cases, your child has not reached mastery level, although he or she may have reached partial mastery.

Needs

Reading
- ◑ Evaluate and Extend Meaning
- ○ Identify Reading Strategies

Vocabulary
- ○ Multimeaning Words

Language
- ◑ Writing Strategies

Language Mechanics
- ○ Writing Conventions

Mathematics
- ◑ Measurement
- ◑ Geometry and Spatial Sense

Mathematics Computation
- ○ Percents

Science
- ○ Earth and Space Science

Social Studies
- ◑ Historical and Cultural Perspectives

Spelling
- No area of needs were identified for this content area

Key ◑ Partial Mastery ○ Non-Mastery

TerraNova

CTBS COMPLETE BATTERY

Home Report

MARY BROWN

Grade 6

Purpose
This page of the Home Report presents information about your child's strengths and needs. This information is provided to help you monitor your child's academic growth.

Simulated Data

Birthdate: 02/08/85
Special Codes:
A B C D E F G H I J K L M N O P Q R S T
3 5 9 7 3 2   1 1 1
Form/Level: A-16
Test Date: 11/01/99   Scoring: PATTERN (IRT)
QM: 08   Norms Date: 1996

Class: PARKER
School: WINFIELD
District: WINFIELD

City/State: WINFIELD, CA

CTB McGraw-Hill   *Page 2*   Copyright © 1997 CTB/McGraw-Hill. All rights reserved.

CTBID:92123B821460001-04-00052-000054
W1 CB HR P2 Final:11/05

Figure 2   (SOURCE: CTB/McGraw-Hill, copyright © 1997. All rights reserved. Reproduced with permission.)

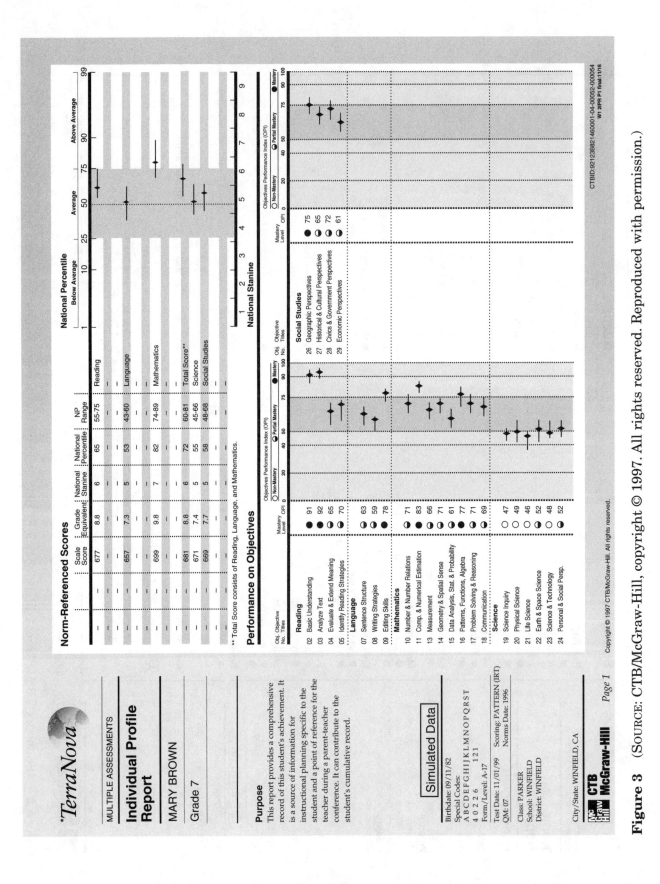

Figure 3 (SOURCE: CTB/McGraw-Hill, copyright © 1997. All rights reserved. Reproduced with permission.)

Observations

Norm-Referenced Scores

The top section of the report presents information about this student's achievement in several different ways. The National Percentile (NP) data and graph indicate how this student performed compared to students of the same grade nationally. The National Percentile range indicates that if this student had taken the test numerous times the scores would have fallen within the range shown. The shaded area on the graph represents the average range of scores, usually defined as the middle 50 percent of students nationally. Scores in the area to the right of the shading are above the average range. Scores in the area to the left of the shading are below the average range.

In Reading, for example, this student achieved a National Percentile rank of 65. This student scored higher than 65 percent of the students nationally. This score is in the average range. This student has a total of five scores in the average range. One score is in the above average range. No scores are in the below average range.

Performance on Objectives

The next section of the report presents performance on the objectives. Each objective is measured by a minimum of 4 items. The Objectives Performance Index (OPI) provides an estimate of the number of items that a student could be expected to answer correctly if there had been 100 items for that objective. The OPI is used to indicate mastery of each objective. An OPI of 75 and above characterizes Mastery. An OPI between 50 and 74 indicates Partial Mastery, and an OPI below 50 indicates Non-Mastery. The two-digit number preceding the objective title identifies the objective, which is fully described in the Teacher's Guide to *TerraNova*. The bands on either side of the diamonds indicate the range within which the student's test scores would fall if the student were tested numerous times.

In Reading, for example, this student could be expected to respond correctly to 91 out of 100 items measuring Basic Understanding. If this student had taken the test numerous times the OPI for this objective would have fallen between 82 and 93.

Teacher Notes

TerraNova

MULTIPLE ASSESSMENTS

Individual Profile Report

MARY BROWN

Grade 7

Purpose

The Observations section of the Individual Profile Report gives teachers and parents information to interpret this report. This page is a narrative description of the data on the other side.

Simulated Data

Birthdate: 09/11/82
Special Codes:
A B C D E F G H I J K L M N O P Q R S T
4 0 2 2 6   1 2 1
Form/Level: A-17
Test Date: 11/01/99   Scoring: PATTERN (IRT)
QM: 08   Norms Date: 1996
Class: PARKER
School: WINFIELD
District: WINFIELD

City/State: WINFIELD, CA

CTB McGraw-Hill   *Page 2*

Figure 4 (SOURCE: CTB/McGraw-Hill, copyright © 1997. All rights reserved. Reproduced with permission.)

TerraNova

MULTIPLE ASSESSMENTS

Student Performance Level Report

KEN ALLEN

Grade 4

Purpose

This report describes this student's achievement in terms of five performance levels for each content area. The meaning of these levels is described on the back of this page. Performance levels are a new way of describing achievement.

Simulated Data

Birthdate: 02/08/86
Special Codes:
A B C D E F G H I J K L M N O P Q R S T
3 5 9 7 3 2   1 1 1
Form/Level: A-14
Test Date: 04/15/97   Scoring: PATTERN (IRT)
QM: 31   Norms Date: 1996
Class: SCHWARZ
School: WINFIELD
District: GREEN VALLEY

City/State: WINFIELD, CA

CTB McGraw-Hill   *Page 1*

Performance Levels	Reading	Language	Mathematics	Science	Social Studies
5 Advanced					
4 Proficient					
3 Nearing Proficiency	✓	✓		✓	✓
2 Progressing	✓	✓	✓	✓	✓
1 Step 1	✓	✓	✓	✓	✓

Partially Proficient

Observations

Performance level scores provide a measure of what students *can do* in terms of the content and skills assessed by *TerraNova*, and typically found in curricula for Grades 3, 4, and 5. It is desirable to work towards achieving a Level 4 (Proficient) or Level 5 (Advanced) by the end of Grade 5.

The number of check marks indicates the performance level this student reached in each content area. For example, this student reached Level 3 in Reading and Social Studies.

The performance level indicates this student can perform the majority of what is described for that level and even more of what is described for the levels below. The student may also be capable of performing some of the things

described in the next higher level, but not enough to have reached that level of performance.

For example, this student can perform the majority of what is described for Level 3 in Reading and even more of what is described for Level 2 and Level 1 in Reading. This student may also be capable of performing some of what is described for Level 4 in Reading.

For each content area look at the skills and knowledge described in the next higher level. These are the competencies this student needs to demonstrate to show academic growth.

Figure 5 (Source: CTB/McGraw-Hill, copyright © 1997. All rights reserved. Reproduced with permission.)

Performance Levels (Grades 3, 4, 5)	Reading	Language	Mathematics	Science	Social Studies
5 Advanced	Students use analogies to generalize. They identify a paraphrase of concepts or ideas in texts. They can indicate thought processes that led them to a previous answer. In written responses, they demonstrate understanding of an implied theme, assess intent of passage information, and provide justification as well as support for their answers.	Students understand logical development in paragraph structure. They identify essential information from notes. They recognize the effect of prepositional phrases on subject-verb agreement. They find and correct at least 4 out of 6 errors when editing simple narratives. They correct run-on and incomplete sentences in more complex texts. They can eliminate all errors when editing their own work.	Students locate decimals on a number line; compute with decimals and fractions; read scale drawings; find areas; identify geometric transformations; construct and label bar graphs; find simple probabilities; find averages; use patterns in data to solve problems; use multiple strategies and concepts to solve unfamiliar problems; express mathematical ideas and explain the problem-solving process.	Students understand a broad range of grade level scientific concepts, such as the structure of Earth and instinctive behavior. They know terminology, such as decomposers, fossil fuel, eclipse, and buoyancy. Knowledge of more complex environmental issues includes, for example, the positive consequences of a forest fire. Students can process and interpret more detailed tables and graphs. They can suggest improvements to experimental design, such as running more trials.	Students consistently demonstrate skills such as synthesizing information from two sources (e.g., a document and a map). They show understanding of the democratic process and global environmental issues, and know the location of continents and major countries. They analyze and summarize information from multiple sources in early American history. They thoroughly explain both sides of an issue and give complete and detailed written answers to questions.
4 Proficient	Students interpret figures of speech. They recognize paraphrase of text information and retrieve information to complete forms. In more complex texts, they identify themes, main ideas, or author purpose/point of view. They analyze and apply information in graphic and text form, make reasonable generalizations, and draw conclusions. In written responses, they can identify key elements from text.	Students select the best supporting sentence for a topic sentence. They use compound predicates to combine sentences. They identify simple subjects and predicates, recognize correct usage when confronted with two types of errors, and find and correct at least 3 out of 6 errors when editing simple narratives. They can edit their own work with only minor errors.	Students compare, order, and round whole numbers; know place value to thousands; identify fractions; use computation and estimation strategies; relate multiplication to addition; measure to nearest half-inch and centimeter; measure and find perimeters; estimate measures; find elapsed times; combine and subdivide shapes; identify parallel lines; interpret tables and graphs; solve two-step problems.	Students have a range of specific science knowledge, including details about animal adaptations and classification, states of matter, and the geology of Earth. They recognize scientific words such as habitat, gravity, and mass. They understand the usefulness of computers. They understand reasons for conserving natural resources. Understanding of experimentation includes analyzing purpose, interpreting data, and selecting tools to gather data.	Students demonstrate skills such as making inferences, using historical documents and analyzing maps to determine the economic strengths of a region. They understand the function of currency in various cultures and supply and demand. They summarize information from multiple sources, recognize relationships, determine relevance of information, and show global awareness. They propose solutions to real-world problems and support ideas with appropriate details.
3 Nearing Proficiency	Students use context clues and structural analysis to determine word meaning. They recognize homonyms and antonyms in grade-level text. They identify important details, sequence, cause and effect, and lessons embedded in the text. They interpret characters' feelings and apply information to new situations. In written responses, they can express an opinion and support it.	Students identify irrelevant sentences in paragraphs and select the best place to insert new information. They recognize faulty sentence construction. They can combine simple sentences with conjunctions and use simple subordination of phrases/clauses. They identify reference sources. They recognize correct conventions for dates, closings, and place names in informal correspondence.	Students identify even and odd numbers; subtract whole numbers with regrouping; multiply and divide by one-digit numbers; identify simple fractions; measure with ruler to nearest inch; tell time to nearest fifteen minutes; recognize and classify common shapes; complete bar graphs; extend numerical and geometric patterns; apply simple logical reasoning.	Students are familiar with the life cycles of plants and animals. They can identify an example of a cold-blooded animal. They infer what once existed from fossil evidence. They understand the water cycle. They know science and society issues such as recycling and sources of pollution. They can sequence technological advances. They extrapolate data, devise a simple classification scheme, and determine the purpose of a simple experiment.	Students demonstrate skills in organizing information. They use time lines, product and global maps, and cardinal directions. They understand simple cause and effect relationships and historical documents. They sequence holidays with events, and associate natural resources. They compare life in different times and understand some economic concepts related to products, jobs, and the environment. They give some detail in written responses.
2 Progressing	Students identify synonyms for grade-level words, and use context clues to define common words. They make simple inferences and predictions based on text. They identify characters' feelings. They can transfer information from text to graphic form, or from graphic form to text. In written responses, they can provide limited support for their answers.	Students identify the use of correct verb tenses and supply verbs to complete sentences. They complete paragraphs by selecting an appropriate topic sentence. They select correct adjective forms.	Students know ordinal numbers; solve coin combination problems; count by tens; add whole numbers with regrouping; have basic estimation skills; understand addition property of zero; write and identify number sentences describing simple situations; read calendars; identify appropriate measurement tools; recognize congruent figures; use simple coordinate grids; read common tables and graphs.	Students recognize that plants decompose and become part of soil. They can classify a plant as a vegetable. They recognize that camouflage relates to survival. They recognize terms such as hibernate. They have an understanding of human impact on the environment and are familiar with causes of pollution. They find the correct bar graph to represent given data and transfer data appropriate for middle elementary grades to a bar graph.	Students demonstrate simple information-processing skills such as using basic maps and keys. They recognize simple geographical terms, types of jobs, modes of transportation, and natural resources. They connect a human need with an appropriate community service. They identify some early famous presidents and know the capital of the United States. Their written answers are partially complete.
1 Step 1	Students select pictured representations of ideas and identify stated details contained in simple texts. In written responses, they can select and transfer information from charts.	Students supply subjects to complete sentences. They identify the correct use of pronouns. They edit for the correct use of end marks and initial capital letters, and identify the correct convention for greetings in letters.	Students read and recognize numbers to 1000; identify real-world use of numbers; add and subtract two-digit numbers without regrouping; identify simple geometric and numerical patterns.	Students recognize basic adaptations for living in the water, identify an animal that is hatched from an egg, and associate an organism with its correct environment. They identify an object as a metal. They have some understanding of conditions on the moon. They supply one way a computer can be useful. They associate an instrument like a telescope with a field of study.	Students are developing fundamental social studies skills such as locating and classifying basic information. They locate information in pictures and read and complete simple bar graphs related to social studies concepts and contexts. They can connect some city buildings with their functions and recognize certain historical objects.

Partially Proficient (levels 3, 2, 1)

W1 SPLR P2:11/02

IMPORTANT: Each performance level, depicted on the other side, indicates the student can perform the majority of what is described for that level and even more of what is described for the levels below. The student may also be capable of performing some of the things described in the next higher level, but not enough to have reached that level.

Figure 6 (SOURCE: CTB/McGraw-Hill, copyright © 1997. All rights reserved. Reproduced with permission.)

confidence interval. In these reports, we usually report either a 90 percent or 95 percent confidence interval. Interpret a confidence interval this way: Suppose we report a 90 percent confidence interval of 25 to 37. This means we estimate that, if the child took the test multiple times, we would expect that child's score to be in the 25 to 37 range 90 percent of the time.

Now look under the section titled Norm-Referenced Scores on the first page of the Individual Profile Report (Figure 3). The farthest column on the right provides the NP Range, which is the National Percentile scores represented by the score bands in the chart.

Next notice the column labeled Grade Equivalent. Theoretically, grade level equivalents equate a student's score in a skill area with the average grade placement of children who made the same score. Many psychologists and test developers would prefer that we stopped reporting grade equivalents, because they can be grossly misleading. For example, the average reading grade level of high school seniors as reported by one of the more popular tests is the eighth grade level. Does that mean that the nation's high school seniors cannot read? No. The way the test publisher calculated grade equivalents was to determine the average test scores for students in grades 4 to 6 and then simply extend the resulting prediction formula to grades 7 to 12. The result is that parents of average high school seniors who take the test in question would mistakenly believe that their seniors are reading four grade levels behind! Stick to the percentile in interpreting your child's scores.

Now look at the columns labeled Scale Score and National Stanine. These are two of a group of scores we also call *standard scores.* In reports for other tests, you may see other standard scores reported, such as Normal Curve Equivalents (NCEs), Z-Scores, and T-Scores. The IQ that we report on intelligence tests, for example, is a standard score. Standard scores are simply a way of expressing a student's scores in terms of the statistical properties of the scores from the norm group against which we are comparing the child. Although most psychologists prefer to speak in terms of standard scores among themselves, parents are advised to stick to percentiles in interpreting your child's performance.

Now look at the section of the report labeled Performance on Objectives. In this section, the test publisher reports how your child did on the various skills that make up each skills area. Note that the scores on each objective are expressed as a percentile band, and you are again told whether your child's score constitutes mastery, non-mastery, or partial mastery. Note that these scores are made up of tallies of sometimes small numbers of test items taken from sections such as Reading or Math. Because they are calculated from a much smaller number of scores than the main scales are (for example, Sentence Comprehension is made up of fewer items than overall Reading), their scores are less reliable than those of the main scales.

Now look at the second page of the Individual Profile Report (Figure 4). Here the test publisher provides a narrative summary of how the child did on the test. These summaries are computer-generated according to rules provided by the publisher. Note that the results descriptions are more general than those on the previous three report pages. But they allow the teacher to form a general picture of which students are performing at what general skill levels.

Finally, your child's guidance counselor may receive a summary report such as the TerraNova Student Performance Level Report. (See Figures 5 and 6.) In this report, the publisher explains to school personnel what skills the test assessed and generally how proficiently the child tested under each skill.

Which States Require Which Tests

Tables 1 through 3 summarize standardized testing practices in the 50 states and the District of Columbia. This information is constantly changing; the information presented here was accurate as of the date of printing of this book. Many states have changed their testing practices in response to revised accountability legislation, while others have changed the tests they use.

Table 1 State Web Sites: Education and Testing

STATE	GENERAL WEB SITE	STATE TESTING WEB SITE
Alabama	http://www.alsde.edu/	http://www.fairtest.org/states/al.htm
Alaska	www.educ.state.ak.us/	http://www.educ.state.ak.us/
Arizona	http://www.ade.state.az.us/	http://www.ade.state.az.us/standards/
Arkansas	http://arkedu.k12.ar.us/	http://www.fairtest.org/states/ar.htm
California	http://goldmine.cde.ca.gov/	http://star.cde.ca.gov/
Colorado	http://www.cde.state.co.us/index_home.htm	http://www.cde.state.co.us/index_assess.htm
Connecticut	http://www.state.ct.us/sde/	http://www.state.ct.us/sde/cmt/index.htm
Delaware	http://www.doe.state.de.us/	http://www.doe.state.de.us/aab/index.htm
District of Columbia	http://www.k12.dc.us/dcps/home.html	http://www.k12.dc.us/dcps/data/data_frame2.html
Florida	http://www.firn.edu/doe/	http://www.firn.edu/doe/sas/sasshome.htm
Georgia	http://www.doe.k12.ga.us/	http://www.doe.k12.ga.us/sla/ret/recotest.html
Hawaii	http://kalama.doe.hawaii.edu/upena/	http://www.fairtest.org/states/hi.htm
Idaho	http://www.sde.state.id.us/Dept/	http://www.sde.state.id.us/instruct/schoolaccount/statetesting.htm
Illinois	http://www.isbe.state.il.us/	http://www.isbe.state.il.us/isat/
Indiana	http://doe.state.in.us/	http://doe.state.in.us/assessment/welcome.html
Iowa	http://www.state.ia.us/educate/index.html	(Tests Chosen Locally)
Kansas	http://www.ksbe.state.ks.us/	http://www.ksbe.state.ks.us/assessment/
Kentucky	htp://www.kde.state.ky.us/	http://www.kde.state.ky.us/oaa/
Louisiana	http://www.doe.state.la.us/DOE/asps/home.asp	http://www.doe.state.la.us/DOE/asps/home.asp?I=HISTAKES
Maine	http://janus.state.me.us/education/homepage.htm	http://janus.state.me.us/education/mea/meacompass.htm
Maryland	http://www.msde.state.md.us/	http://msp.msde.state.md.us/
Massachusetts	http://www.doe.mass.edu/	http://www.doe.mass.edu/mcas/
Michigan	http://www.mde.state.mi.us/	http://www.MeritAward.state.mi.us/merit/meap/index.htm

STATE	GENERAL WEB SITE	STATE TESTING WEB SITE
Minnesota	http://www.educ.state.mn.us/	http://fairtest.org/states/mn.htm
Mississippi	http://mdek12.state.ms.us/	http://fairtest.org/states/ms.htm
Missouri	http://services.dese.state.mo.us/	http://fairtest.org/states/mo.htm
Montana	http://www.metnet.state.mt.us/	http://fairtest.org/states/mt.htm
Nebraska	http://www.nde.state.ne.us/	http://www.edneb.org/IPS/AppAccrd/ApprAccrd.html
Nevada	http://www.nde.state.nv.us/	http://www.nsn.k12.nv.us/nvdoe/reports/TerraNova.doc
New Hampshire	http://www.state.nh.us/doe/	http://www.state.nh.us/doe/Assessment/assessme(NHEIAP).htm
New Jersey	http://www.state.nj.us/education/	http://www.state.nj.us/njded/stass/index.html
New Mexico	http://sde.state.nm.us/	http://sde.state.nm.us/press/august30a.html
New York	http://www.nysed.gov/	http://www.emsc.nysed.gov/ciai/assess.html
North Carolina	http://www.dpi.state.nc.us/	http://www.dpi.state.nc.us/accountability/reporting/index.html
North Dakota	http://www.dpi.state.nd.us/dpi/index.htm	http://www.dpi.state.nd.us/dpi/reports/assess/assess.htm
Ohio	http://www.ode.state.oh.us/	http://www.ode.state.oh.us/ca/
Oklahoma	http://sde.state.ok.us/	http://sde.state.ok.us/acrob/testpack.pdf
Oregon	http://www.ode.state.or.us//	http://www.ode.state.or.us//asmt/index.htm
Pennsylvania	http://www.pde.psu.edu/	http://www.fairtest.org/states/pa.htm
Rhode Island	http://www.ridoe.net/	http://www.ridoe.net/standards/default.htm
South Carolina	http://www.state.sc.us/sde/	http://www.state.sc.us/sde/reports/terranov.htm
South Dakota	http://www.state.sd.us/state/executive/deca/	http://www.state.sd.us/state/executive/deca/TA/McRelReport/McRelReports.htm
Tennessee	http://www.state.tn.us/education/	http://www.state.tn.us/education/tsintro.htm
Texas	http://www.tea.state.tx.us/	http://www.tea.state.tx.us/student.assessment/
Utah	http://www.usoe.k12.ut.us/	http://www.usoe.k12.ut.us/eval/usoeeval.htm
Vermont	http://www.state.vt.us/educ/	http://www.fairtest.org/states/vt.htm

STATE	GENERAL WEB SITE	STATE TESTING WEB SITE
Virginia	http://www.pen.k12.va.us/Anthology/VDOE/	http://www.pen.k12.va.us/VDOE/Assessment/home.shtml
Washington	http://www.k12.wa.us/	http://www.k12.wa.us/assessment/
West Virginia	http://wvde.state.wv.us/	http://wvde.state.wv.us/
Wisconsin	http://www.dpi.state.wi.us/	http://www.dpi.state.wi.us/dpi/dltcl/eis/achfacts.html
Wyoming	http://www.k12.wy.us/wdehome.html	http://www.asme.com/wycas/index.htm

Table 2 Norm-Referenced and Criterion-Referenced Tests Administered by State

STATE	NORM-REFERENCED TEST	CRITERION-REFERENCED TEST	EXIT EXAM
Alabama	Stanford Achievement Test		Alabama High School Graduation Exam
Alaska	California Achievement Test	Alaska Benchmark Examinations	
Arizona	Stanford Achievement Test	Arizona's Instrument to Measure Standards (AIMS)	
Arkansas	Stanford Achievement Test		
California	Stanford Achievement Test	Standardized Testing and Reporting Supplement	High School Exit Exam (HSEE)
Colorado	None	Colorado Student Assessment Program	
Connecticut		Connecticut Mastery Test	
Delaware	Stanford Achievement Test	Delaware Student Testing Program	
District of Columbia	Stanford Achievement Test		
Florida	(Locally Selected)	Florida Comprehensive Assessment Test (FCAT)	High School Competency Test (HSCT)
Georgia	Stanford Achievement Test	Georgia Kindergarten Assessment Program—Revised and Criterion-Referenced Competency Tests (CRCT)	Georgia High School Graduation Tests
Hawaii	Stanford Achievement Test	Credit by Examination	Hawaii State Test of Essential Competencies
Idaho	Iowa Tests of Basic Skills/ Tests of Achievement and Proficiency	Direct Writing/Mathematics Assessment, Idaho Reading Indicator	
Illinois		Illinois Standards Achievement Tests	Prairie State Achievement Examination
Indiana		Indiana Statewide Testing for Educational Progress	
Iowa	(None)		
Kansas		(State-Developed Tests)	
Kentucky	Comprehensive Test of Basic Skills	Kentucky Core Content Tests	
Louisiana	Iowa Tests of Basic Skills	Louisiana Educational Assessment Program	Graduate Exit Exam
Maine		Maine Educational Assessment	High School Assessment Test
Maryland		Maryland School Performance Assessment Program, Maryland Functional Testing Program	

STATE	NORM-REFERENCED TEST	CRITERION-REFERENCED TEST	EXIT EXAM
Massachusetts		Massachusetts Comprehensive Assessment System	
Michigan		Michigan Educational Assessment Program	High School Test
Minnesota		Basic Standards Test	Profile of Learning
Mississippi	Comprehensive Test of Basic Skills	Subject Area Testing Program	Functional Literacy Examination
Missouri		Missouri Mastery and Achievement Test	
Montana	Iowa Tests of Basic Skills		
Nebraska			
Nevada	TerraNova		Nevada High School Proficiency Examination
New Hampshire		NH Educational Improvement and Assessment Program	
New Jersey		Elementary School Proficiency Test/Early Warning Test	High School Proficiency Test
New Mexico	TerraNova		New Mexico High School Competency Exam
New York		Pupil Evaluation Program/ Preliminary Competency Tests	Regents Competency Tests
North Carolina	Iowa Tests of Basic Skills	NC End of Grade Test	
North Dakota	TerraNova	ND Reading, Writing, Speaking, Listening, Math Test	
Ohio		Ohio Proficiency Tests	Ohio Proficiency Tests
Oklahoma	Iowa Tests of Basic Skills	Oklahoma Criterion- Referenced Tests	
Oregon		Oregon Statewide Assessment	
Pennsylvania		Pennsylvania System of School Assessment	
Rhode Island	Metropolitan Achievement Test	New Standards English Language Arts Reference Exam, New Standards Mathematics Reference Exam, Rhode Island Writing Assessment, and Rhode Island Health Education Assessment	
South Carolina	TerraNova	Palmetto Achievement Challenge Tests	High School Exit Exam
South Dakota	Stanford Achievement Test		
Tennessee	Tennessee Comprehensive Assessment Program	Tennessee Comprehensive Assessment Program	

STATE	NORM-REFERENCED TEST	CRITERION-REFERENCED TEST	EXIT EXAM
Texas		Texas Assessment of Academic Skills, End-of-Course Examinations	Texas Assessment of Academic Skills
Utah	Stanford Achievement Test	Core Curriculum Testing	
Vermont		New Standards Reference Exams	
Virginia	Stanford Achievement Test	Virginia Standards of Learning	Virginia Standards of Learning
Washington	Iowa Tests of Basic Skills	Washington Assessment of Student Learning	Washington Assessment of Student Learning
West Virginia	Stanford Achievement Test		
Wisconsin	TerraNova	Wisconsin Knowledge and Concepts Examinations	
Wyoming	TerraNova	Wyoming Comprehensive Assessment System	Wyoming Comprehensive Assessment System

Table 3   Standardized Test Schedules by State

STATE	KG	1	2	3	4	5	6	7	8	9	10	11	12	COMMENT
Alabama				X	X	X	X	X	X	X	X	X	X	
Alaska				X	X		X		X			X		
Arizona			X	X	X	X	X	X	X	X	X	X	X	
Arkansas					X	X		X	X		X	X	X	
California			X	X	X	X	X	X	X	X	X	X		
Colorado				X	X	X		X	X					
Connecticut					X		X		X					
Delaware				X	X	X			X		X	X		
District of Columbia		X	X	X	X	X	X	X	X	X	X	X		
Florida				X	X	X			X		X			There is no state-mandated norm-referenced testing. However, the state collects information furnished by local districts that elect to perform norm-referenced testing. The FCAT is administered to Grades 4, 8, and 10 to assess reading and Grades 5, 8, and 10 to assess math.
Georgia	X			X	X	X	X		X			X		
Hawaii				X			X		X		X			The Credit by Examination is voluntary and is given in Grade 8 in Algebra and Foreign Languages.
Idaho				X	X	X	X	X	X	X	X	X		
Illinois				X	X	X		X	X		X	X		Exit Exam failure will not disqualify students from graduation if all other requirements are met.
Indiana				X			X		X		X			
Iowa		*	*	*	*	*	*	*	*	*	*	*	*	*Iowa does not currently have a statewide testing program. Locally chosen assessments are administered to grades determined locally.
Kansas				X	X	X		X	X		X	X		

STATE	KG	1	2	3	4	5	6	7	8	9	10	11	12	COMMENT
Kentucky					X	X	X	X	X	X	X	X	X	
Louisiana				X	X	X	X	X	X	X	X	X	X	
Maine					X				X			X		
Maryland				X		X			X	X	X	X	X	
Massachusetts				X	X	X		X	X	X	X			
Michigan					X	X		X	X					
Minnesota				X		X			X	X	X	X	X	
Mississippi				X	X	X	X	X	X					Mississippi officials would not return phone calls or emails regarding this information.
Missouri			X	X	X	X	X	X	X	X	X			
Montana					X				X			X		The State Board of Education has decided to use a single norm-referenced test statewide beginning 2000–2001 school year.
Nebraska		**	**	**	**	**	**	**	**	**	**	**	**	**Decisions regarding testing are left to the individual school districts.
Nevada					X				X					Districts choose whether and how to test with norm-referenced tests.
New Hampshire				X			X				X			
New Jersey				X	X			X	X	X	X	X		
New Mexico					X		X		X					
New York				X	X	X	X	X	X	X			X	Assessment program is going through major revisions.
North Carolina	X			X	X	X	X		X	X			X	NRT Testing selects samples of students, not all.
North Dakota					X		X		X		X			
Ohio					X		X			X			X	
Oklahoma				X		X		X	X			X		
Oregon				X		X			X		X			

STATE	KG	1	2	3	4	5	6	7	8	9	10	11	12	COMMENT
Pennsylvania						X	X		X	X		X		
Rhode Island				X	X	X		X	X	X	X	X		
South Carolina				X	X	X	X	X	X	X	X	***	***	***Students who fail the High School Exit Exam have opportunities to take the exam again in grades 11 and 12.
South Dakota			X		X	X				X	X		X		
Tennessee			X	X	X	X	X	X	X						
Texas				X	X	X	X	X	X			X	X	X	
Utah		X	X	X	X	X	X	X	X	X	X	X	X	
Vermont					X	X	X		X	X	X	X		Rated by the Centers for Fair and Open Testing as a nearly model system for assessment.
Virginia				X	X	X	X		X	X		X		
Washington					X			X			X			
West Virginia				X	X	X	X	X	X	X	X	X		
Wisconsin					X				X		X			
Wyoming					X				X			X		

Testing Accommodations

The more testing procedures vary from one classroom or school to the next, the less we can compare the scores from one group to another. Consider a test in which the publisher recommends that three sections of the test be given in one 45-minute session per day on three consecutive days. School A follows those directions. To save time, School B gives all three sections of the test in one session lasting slightly more than two hours. We can't say that both schools followed the same testing procedures. Remember that the test publishers provide testing procedures so schools can administer the tests in as close a manner as possible to the way the tests were administered to the groups used to obtain test norms. When we compare students' scores to norms, we want to compare apples to apples, not apples to oranges.

Most schools justifiably resist making any changes in testing procedures. Informally, a teacher can make minor changes that don't alter the testing procedures, such as separating two students who talk with each other instead of paying attention to the test; letting Lisa, who is getting over an ear infection, sit closer to the front so she can hear better; or moving Jeffrey away from the window to prevent his looking out the window and daydreaming.

There are two groups of students who require more formal testing accommodations. One group of students is identified as having a disability under Section 504 of the Rehabilitation Act of 1973 (Public Law 93-112). These students face

some challenge but, with reasonable and appropriate accommodation, can take advantage of the same educational opportunities as other students. That is, they have a condition that requires some accommodation for them.

Just as schools must remove physical barriers to accommodate students with disabilities, they must make appropriate accommodations to remove other types of barriers to students' access to education. Marie is profoundly deaf, even with strong hearing aids. She does well in school with the aid of an interpreter, who signs her teacher's instructions to her and tells her teacher what Marie says in reply. An appropriate accommodation for Marie would be to provide the interpreter to sign test instructions to her, or to allow her to watch a videotape with an interpreter signing test instructions. Such a reasonable accommodation would not deviate from standard testing procedures and, in fact, would ensure that Marie received the same instructions as the other students.

If your child is considered disabled and has what is generally called a Section 504 Plan or individual accommodation plan (IAP), then the appropriate way to ask for testing accommodations is to ask for them in a meeting to discuss school accommodations under the plan. If your child is not already covered by such a plan, he or she won't qualify for one merely because you request testing accommodations.

The other group of students who may receive formal testing accommodations are those identified as handicapped under the Individuals with Disabilities Education Act (IDEA)—students with mental retardation, learning disabilities, serious emotional disturbance, orthopedic handicap, hearing or visual problems, and other handicaps defined in the law. These students have been identified under procedures governed by federal and sometimes state law, and their education is governed by a document called the Individualized Educational Program (IEP). Unless you are under a court order specifically revoking your educational rights on behalf of your child, you are a full member of the IEP team even if you and your child's other parent are divorced and the other parent has custody. Until recently, IEP teams actually had the prerogative to exclude certain handicapped students from taking standardized group testing altogether. However, today states make it more difficult to exclude students from testing.

If your child is classified as handicapped and has an IEP, the appropriate place to ask for testing accommodations is in an IEP team meeting. In fact, federal regulations require IEP teams to address testing accommodations. You have the right to call a meeting at any time. In that meeting, you will have the opportunity to present your case for the accommodations you believe are necessary. Be prepared for the other team members to resist making extreme accommodations unless you can present a very strong case. If your child is identified as handicapped and you believe that he or she should be provided special testing accommodations, contact the person at your child's school who is responsible for convening IEP meetings and request a meeting to discuss testing accommodations.

Problems arise when a request is made for accommodations that cause major departures from standard testing procedures. For example, Lynn has an identified learning disability in mathematics calculation and attends resource classes for math. Her disability is so severe that her IEP calls for her to use a calculator when performing all math problems. She fully under-

stands math concepts, but she simply can't perform the calculations without the aid of a calculator. Now it's time for Lynn to take the school-based standardized tests, and she asks to use a calculator. In this case, since her IEP already requires her to be provided with a calculator when performing math calculations, she may be allowed a calculator during school standardized tests. However, because using a calculator constitutes a major violation of standard testing procedures, her score on all sections in which she is allowed to use a calculator will be recorded as a failure, and her results in some states will be removed from among those of other students in her school in calculating school results.

How do we determine whether a student is allowed formal accommodations in standardized school testing and what these accommodations may be? First, if your child is not already identified as either handicapped or disabled, having the child classified in either group solely to receive testing accommodations will be considered a violation of the laws governing both classifications. Second, even if your child is already classified in either group, your state's department of public instruction will provide strict guidelines for the testing accommodations schools may make. Third, even if your child is classified in either group and you are proposing testing accommodations allowed under state testing guidelines, any accommodations must still be both *reasonable* and *appropriate*. To be reasonable and appropriate, testing accommodations must relate to your child's disability and must be similar to those already in place in his or her daily educational program. If your child is always tested individually in a separate room for all tests in all subjects, then a similar practice in taking school-based standardized tests may be appropriate. But if your child has a learning disability only in mathematics calculation, requesting that all test questions be read to him or her is inappropriate because that accommodation does not relate to his identified handicap.

Glossary

Accountability   The idea that a school district is held responsible for the achievement of its students. The term may also be applied to holding students responsible for a certain level of achievement in order to be promoted or to graduate.

Achievement test   An assessment that measures current knowledge in one or more of the areas taught in most schools, such as reading, math, and language arts.

Aptitude test   An assessment designed to predict a student's potential for learning knowledge or skills.

Content validity   The extent to which a test represents the content it is designed to cover.

Criterion-referenced test   A test that rates how thoroughly a student has mastered a specific skill or area of knowledge. Typically, a criterion-referenced test is subjective, and relies on someone to observe and rate student work; it doesn't allow for easy comparisons of achievement among students. Performance assessments are criterion-referenced tests. The opposite of a criterion-referenced test is a norm-referenced test.

Frequency distribution   A tabulation of individual scores (or groups of scores) that shows the number of persons who obtained each score.

Generalizability   The idea that the score on a test reflects what a child knows about a subject, or how well he performs the skills the test is supposed to be assessing. Generalizability requires that enough test items are administered to truly assess a student's achievement.

Grade equivalent   A score on a scale developed to indicate the school grade (usually measured in months of a year) that corresponds to an average chronological age, mental age, test score, or other characteristic. A grade equivalent of 6.4 is interpreted as a score that is average for a group in the fourth month of Grade 6.

High-stakes assessment   A type of standardized test that has major consequences for a student or school (such as whether a child graduates from high school or gets admitted to college).

Mean   Average score of a group of scores.

Median   The middle score in a set of scores ranked from smallest to largest.

National percentile   Percentile score derived from the performance of a group of individuals across the nation.

Normative sample   A comparison group consisting of individuals who have taken a test under standard conditions.

Norm-referenced test A standardized test that can compare scores of students in one school with a reference group (usually other students in the same grade and age, called the "norm group"). Norm-referenced tests compare the achievement of one student or the students of a school, school district, or state with the norm score.

Norms A summary of the performance of a group of individuals on which a test was standardized.

Percentile An incorrect form of the word *centile*, which is the percent of a group of scores that falls below a given score. Although the correct term is *centile*, much of the testing literature has adopted the term *percentile*.

Performance standards A level of performance on a test set by education experts.

Quartiles Points that divide the frequency distribution of scores into equal fourths.

Regression to the mean The tendency of scores in a group of scores to vary in the direction of the mean. For example: If a child has an abnormally low score on a test, she is likely to make a higher score (that is, one closer to the mean) the next time she takes the test.

Reliability The consistency with which a test measures some trait or characteristic. A measure can be reliable without being valid, but it can't be valid without being reliable.

Standard deviation A statistical measure used to describe the extent to which scores vary in a group of scores. Approximately 68 percent of scores in a group are expected to be in a range from one standard deviation below the mean to one standard deviation above the mean.

Standardized test A test that contains well-defined questions of proven validity and that produces reliable scores. Such tests are commonly paper-and-pencil exams containing multiple-choice items, true or false questions, matching exercises, or short fill-in-the-blanks items. These tests may also include performance assessment items (such as a writing sample), but assessment items cannot be completed quickly or scored reliably.

Test anxiety Anxiety that occurs in test-taking situations. Test anxiety can seriously impair individuals' ability to obtain accurate scores on a test.

Validity The extent to which a test measures the trait or characteristic it is designed to measure. Also see *reliability*.

Answer Keys for Practice Skills

Chapter 2: Basic Facts

1	A
2	B
3	C
4	D
5	A
6	B
7	C
8	D
9	A
10	A
11	D
12	B
13	B
14	C
15	D
16	B
17	C
18	C
19	D
20	A
21	A
22	C
23	D
24	A
25	D
26	A

Chapter 3: Numeration

1	A
2	B
3	C
4	B
5	D
6	C
7	B
8	A
9	D
10	C
11	B
12	C
13	D
14	C
15	A
16	D
17	B
18	A
19	C
20	D
21	A
22	B
23	C
24	A
25	B

Chapter 4: Two-Digit Addition and Subtraction

1	C
2	B
3	A
4	D
5	D
6	D
7	C
8	C
9	A
10	A
11	B
12	D
13	D
14	D
15	D
16	C
17	B
18	A
19	D
20	C

Chapter 5: Time: Clocks and Calendars

1	D
2	B
3	A
4	D
5	C
6	B
7	D
8	B
9	D
10	C
11	A
12	B
13	D
14	C
15	D
16	B

Chapter 6: Money

1	D
2	C
3	B
4	A
5	D
6	C
7	D
8	B
9	A
10	C
11	C
12	B

Chapter 7: Measurement

1	D
2	C
3	C
4	B
5	C
6	D
7	A
8	A
9	C
10	B
11	B
12	A
13	A
14	C
15	D

Chapter 8: Geometry

1	A
2	C
3	A
4	C
5	D
6	C
7	B
8	D
9	C

Chapter 9: Fractions

1	A
2	C
3	C
4	D
5	B
6	C
7	B
8	D
9	B
10	C
11	A
12	D
13	D
14	A

Chapter 10: Multiplication and More

1	B
2	C
3	D
4	A
5	B
6	D
7	C
8	C
9	B
10	C
11	B
12	D

Sample Practice Test

You may be riding a roller coaster of feelings and opinions at this point. If your child has gone through the preceding chapters easily, then you're both probably excited to move on, to jump in with both feet, take the test, and that will be that. On the other hand, your child may have struggled a bit with some of the chapters. Some of the concepts may be difficult for him and will require a little more practice. Never fear! All children acquire skills in all areas of learning when they are developmentally ready. We can't push them, but we can reinforce the skills that they already know. In addition, we can play games and do activities to pave the way for their understanding of the skills that they will need to master later. With luck, that's what you've done with the preceding chapters.

The test that follows is designed to incorporate components of several different kinds of standardized tests. The test that your child takes in school probably won't look just like this one, but it should be sufficiently similar so that he should be pretty comfortable with the format. The administration of tests varies as well, so the part you play in this practice testing will take several different shapes.

First, many items on standardized tests in second grade are read by the teacher, so listening skills are crucial. For this reason, this practice test was designed to be *read to* your child by you. The copy of the test that your child uses will have very few directions written on it. There will be a few items where your child has the directions to serve as a reminder, but those questions also should be read by you. It is important that your child hear the rhythm and language used in standardized tests, aiding in familiarizing him with the whole process. If you wish, you may have your child read the directions that precede each test section to you first and explain what he thinks the item is asking him to do. He may try it on his own if you feel he understands it, or you may want to clarify the instructions.

As in a real test, there are about 60 math questions or items to complete.

Test Administration

This test has been arranged into three sessions, allowing for breaks and rest periods. If you like, you may complete the entire test in one day, but it is not recommended that your child attempt to finish it in one sitting. As test administrator, you'll find that you'll need to stretch, have a snack, or use the bathroom too! If you plan to do the test in one day, leave at least 15 minutes between sessions.

Before you start, prepare a quiet place, free of distractions. Have two or three sharpened pencils with erasers that don't smudge, a flat, clear work space, this copy of directions for administering the test, and your child's copy of the test carefully removed from the book. As you proceed from item to item, be sure that your child is looking at the same spot you are, and encourage him to ask you if he doesn't understand something. In a real testing situation, questions are accepted, but the extent to which items can be explained is limited. Don't go

MATH, GRADE TWO: GET READY!

overboard in making sure your second grader understands what to do. He'll have to learn to trust his instincts somewhat. The test shouldn't take all day. If your youngster seems to be dawdling along, enforce time limits and help him to understand that the real test will have time limits as well.

PARENT SCRIPT FOR SAMPLE PRACTICE TEST

Session One (Test Administrator's Version, 30–40 minutes)

1   How many baseballs are there?

2   Choose the math problem that shows what is happening in the picture.

3   Choose the fact that belongs to the fact family shown.

4   Look at the fact shown, 14 − 8 = 6. Choose the related fact.

5   Choose the fact family that matches the picture shown.

6   Look at the math sentence. Choose the correct answer.

7   Look at the math sentence. Choose the missing addend.

8   Read this math story to yourself as I read it aloud. Jed caught 4 grasshoppers. Then he caught 6 crickets. How many bugs does he have now? Choose the math sentence that best matches the story.

9   Look at the number. Notice that the number 5 is underlined. Choose the value of the 5 in the number 58.

10   Do the same thing in number 10. Notice that in the number 659, the number 6 is underlined. Choose the value of that number 6.

11   Look at the picture of math models. You need to find the numeral represented by the models. Now look at the choices A, B, C, and D. The answer D says, "None of the above." This means that perhaps the answer to the question is not one of the choices. If this is true, mark D, "None of the above." If you can find the correct answer, choose that one.

12   Look at the numbers shown. They show a pattern. Choose the numbers that continue the pattern.

13   Look at the list of numbers. One of the numbers is missing. Choose the missing number.

14   Choose the symbol that will make the number sentence true.

15   Choose the shape that is ninth in line.

16   Look at the items numbered 16 to 25. These math problems may require you to do some work on another piece of paper. Do not write on the test itself. Instead, do all your figuring on the extra piece of paper you were given. When you have figured out the answer, find it on the test, and fill in the answer sheet. If an answer space has the letters "NG" next to it, the "NG" stands for "not given." If you figure out an answer but you can't find it among the choices, you may need to mark "NG" because the answer is not given.

Do the next 10 problems on your own. Use the extra paper whenever you need it. Stop when you get to the stop sign. You may begin. [Allow 15 minutes for this section.]

Session Two (Test Administrator's Version, 20–30 minutes)

26   Look at the clock next to the number 26. Choose the numbers that show the correct time.

27   Look at the clock next to the number 27. Choose the clock that shows what the time would be 2 hours later.

28   Look at the clock next to the number 28. Choose the time that shows 3 hours earlier.

29   Look at the clock in the next item. Read the time given. Choose the numbers that show that time.

30   Listen carefully, and follow along as I read the word problem. Amy has dance lessons at 5:00. It takes 15 minutes to get there. The

clock shows the time right now. What time will she get to her dance lesson?

31 Look at the group of coins. Choose the amount shown in the picture.

32 Look at the two groups of coins. Decide which group has the smallest amount, and choose that amount.

33 The jacks in the picture cost 65 cents. If you pay $1, how much change will you get back?

34 Look at the four groups of coins. Choose the group that has the most money.

35 Listen carefully, and follow along as I read the story problem. Adam wants to buy some football cards that cost $0.75 (75 cents). The picture shows how much money he has. How much more money does Adam need to buy cards?

36 Move down to the ruler and the stick. Choose the correct measurement.

37 Here is a mug of hot chocolate. Choose the best estimate telling how much the mug holds.

38 Look at the thermometer. Choose the correct temperature shown.

39 Move down to the pint container. Choose another way to show the same amount.

40 How many units are shown in this rectangle?

41 This is a can of tennis balls. Which word names the shape of the can?

42 If you traced around the can of tennis balls, which shape would you see?

43 Choose the cylinder.

44 Choose the figure that shows a line of symmetry.

45 Look at the square. Notice the macaroni outside the square. How many macaroni will it take to measure the perimeter of the square?

Session Three (Test Administrator's Version, 15 minutes)

46 Look at the fraction in the box. Choose the picture that shows that fraction.

47 Look at the picture. Choose the fraction that matches the picture.

48 Move down to the hearts, and listen closely. Choose the fraction that shows how many gray hearts there are.

49 Look at the picture of the frogs. Choose the problem that matches the picture.

Cut along dashed line.

To the Student:

These tests will give you a chance to put the tips you have learned to work.
  A few last reminders . . .

- Be sure you understand all the directions before you begin each test. You may ask the teacher questions about the directions if you do not understand them.

- Work as quickly as you can during each test.

- When you change an answer, be sure to erase your first mark completely.

- You can guess at an answer or skip difficult items and go back to them later.

- Use the tips you have learned whenever you can.

- It is OK to be a little nervous. You may even do better.

Now that you have completed the lessons in this book, you are on your way to scoring high!

Cut along dashed line.

STUDENT'S NAME		SCHOOL
LAST	FIRST	MI	TEACHER

FEMALE ◯   MALE ◯

BIRTHDATE

MONTH	DAY	YEAR

JAN ◯ FEB ◯ MAR ◯ APR ◯ MAY ◯ JUN ◯ JUL ◯ AUG ◯ SEP ◯ OCT ◯ NOV ◯ DEC ◯

GRADE

① ② ③ ④ ⑤ ⑥

Session One

1 Ⓐ Ⓑ Ⓒ Ⓓ   6 Ⓐ Ⓑ Ⓒ Ⓓ   10 Ⓐ Ⓑ Ⓒ Ⓓ   14 Ⓐ Ⓑ Ⓒ Ⓓ   18 Ⓐ Ⓑ Ⓒ Ⓓ   22 Ⓐ Ⓑ Ⓒ Ⓓ
2 Ⓐ Ⓑ Ⓒ Ⓓ   7 Ⓐ Ⓑ Ⓒ Ⓓ   11 Ⓐ Ⓑ Ⓒ Ⓓ   15 Ⓐ Ⓑ Ⓒ Ⓓ   19 Ⓐ Ⓑ Ⓒ Ⓓ   23 Ⓐ Ⓑ Ⓒ Ⓓ
3 Ⓐ Ⓑ Ⓒ Ⓓ   8 Ⓐ Ⓑ Ⓒ Ⓓ   12 Ⓐ Ⓑ Ⓒ Ⓓ   16 Ⓐ Ⓑ Ⓒ Ⓓ   20 Ⓐ Ⓑ Ⓒ Ⓓ   24 Ⓐ Ⓑ Ⓒ Ⓓ
4 Ⓐ Ⓑ Ⓒ Ⓓ   9 Ⓐ Ⓑ Ⓒ Ⓓ   13 Ⓐ Ⓑ Ⓒ Ⓓ   17 Ⓐ Ⓑ Ⓒ Ⓓ   21 Ⓐ Ⓑ Ⓒ Ⓓ   25 Ⓐ Ⓑ Ⓒ Ⓓ
5 Ⓐ Ⓑ Ⓒ Ⓓ

Session Two

26 Ⓐ Ⓑ Ⓒ Ⓓ   30 Ⓐ Ⓑ Ⓒ Ⓓ   34 Ⓐ Ⓑ Ⓒ Ⓓ   37 Ⓐ Ⓑ Ⓒ Ⓓ   40 Ⓐ Ⓑ Ⓒ Ⓓ   43 Ⓐ Ⓑ Ⓒ Ⓓ
27 Ⓐ Ⓑ Ⓒ Ⓓ   31 Ⓐ Ⓑ Ⓒ Ⓓ   35 Ⓐ Ⓑ Ⓒ Ⓓ   38 Ⓐ Ⓑ Ⓒ Ⓓ   41 Ⓐ Ⓑ Ⓒ Ⓓ   44 Ⓐ Ⓑ Ⓒ Ⓓ
28 Ⓐ Ⓑ Ⓒ Ⓓ   32 Ⓐ Ⓑ Ⓒ Ⓓ   36 Ⓐ Ⓑ Ⓒ Ⓓ   39 Ⓐ Ⓑ Ⓒ Ⓓ   42 Ⓐ Ⓑ Ⓒ Ⓓ   45 Ⓐ Ⓑ Ⓒ Ⓓ
29 Ⓐ Ⓑ Ⓒ Ⓓ   33 Ⓐ Ⓑ Ⓒ Ⓓ

Session Three

46 Ⓐ Ⓑ Ⓒ Ⓓ   47 Ⓐ Ⓑ Ⓒ Ⓓ   48 Ⓐ Ⓑ Ⓒ Ⓓ   49 Ⓐ Ⓑ Ⓒ Ⓓ

Cut along dashed line.

SESSION ONE
(STUDENT'S VERSION)

1 **A** 13   **B** 15

   C 16   **D** 17

2 **A** 7 + 3 = 10

   B 10 − 3 = 7

   C 10 − 7 = 3

   D 12 − 9 = 3

3 6 + 5 = 11   11 − 5 = 6
   11 − 6 = 5

   A 11 + 5 = 16

   B 6 − 5 = 1

   C 5 + 6 = 11

   D 11 − 4 = 7

4 14 − 8 = 6

   A 7 + 7 = 14

   B 8 − 6 = 2

   C 8 + 6 = 14

   D 2 + 6 = 8

5 **A** 3 + 4 = 7   4 + 3 = 7
      7 − 3 = 4   7 − 4 = 3

   B 7 + 5 = 12   5 + 7 = 12
      12 − 5 = 7   12 − 7 = 5

   C 2 + 10 = 12   10 + 2 = 12
      12 − 10 = 2   12 − 2 = 10

   D 7 + 3 = 10   3 + 7 = 10
      10 − 7 = 3   10 − 3 = 7

6 6 − 4 = ___

   A 2

   B 3

   C 5

   D 10

GO

Cut along dashed line.

7 $7 + \underline{\quad} = 13$

   A 5

   B 6

   C 7

   D 11

---

8 Jed caught 4 grasshoppers. Then he caught 6 crickets. How many bugs does he have now?

   A $6 - 4 = 2$

   B $2 + 4 = 6$

   C $4 + 6 = 10$

   D $10 - 6 = 4$

---

9 <u>5</u>8

   A 5

   B 50

   C 500

   D 5000

---

10 <u>6</u>59

   A 6

   B 60

   C 600

   D 6000

---

11 8 tens, 4 ones

   A 84

   B 48

   C 804

   D none of the above

---

12 20, 25, 30, 35, 40, __, __, __, __

   A 41, 42, 43, 44

   B 39, 38, 37, 36

   C 50, 60, 70, 80

   D 45, 50, 55, 60

---

13 10, 12, 14, 16, __, 20, 22

   A 17

   B 15

   C 19

   D 18

---

14 46 ___ 63

   A >

   B <

   C +

   D =

Cut along dashed line

GO

☆ ☾ ⬜ ◯ ▭ ◯ △ ▱ ◇ ▱

15 **A** ☆   **B** ◯

 C ◇   **D** △

16   25
 +34

 A 59   **B** 95

 C 77   **D** 11

17   52
 +16

 A 44

 B 68

 C 77

 D 35

18 28 + 48 = ___

 A 66

 B 102

 C 76

 D 20

19 39 + 28 = ___

 A 57

 B 51

 C 11

 D 67

20 85 − 52 = ___

 A 37

 B 13

 C 33

 D NG

21 74 − 28 = ___

 A 54

 B 46

 C 94

 D 96

22 51 − 19 = ___

 A 48

 B 32

 C 60

 D 70

GO

23   456
        +123

    A 579

    B 333

    C 379

    D 573

---

24 Tomico had 24 marbles. She got 9 more for her birthday. How many marbles does she have?

    A 15

    B 74

    C 35

    D 33

---

25 There were 33 birds at the bird feeder. A cat scared 10 birds away. How many birds were left at the feeder?

    A 43

    B 22

    C 23

    D 61

Cut along dashed line.

SESSION TWO
(STUDENT'S VERSION)

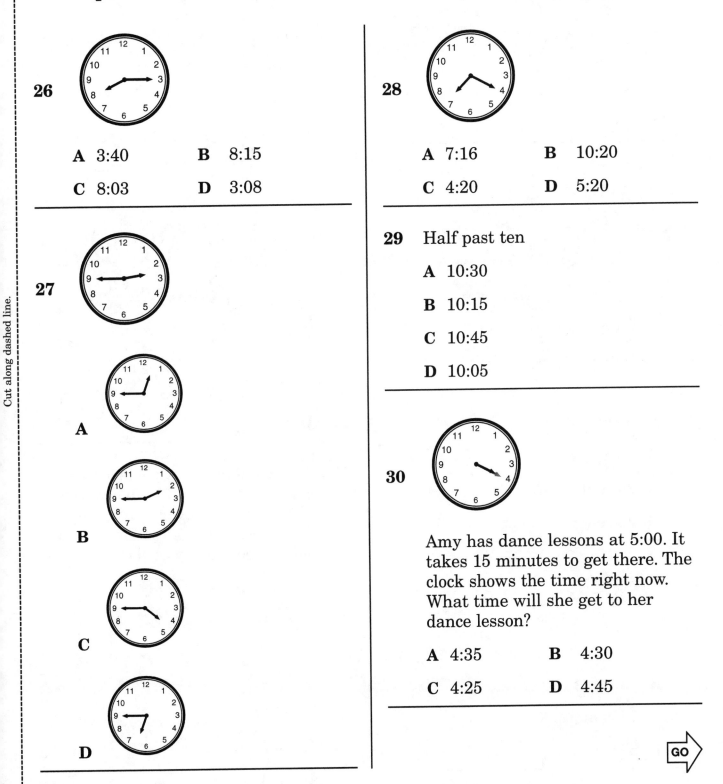

26

A   3:40   B   8:15

C   8:03   D   3:08

27

A

B

C

D

28

A   7:16   B   10:20

C   4:20   D   5:20

29   Half past ten

A   10:30

B   10:15

C   10:45

D   10:05

30

Amy has dance lessons at 5:00. It takes 15 minutes to get there. The clock shows the time right now. What time will she get to her dance lesson?

A   4:35   B   4:30

C   4:25   D   4:45

GO

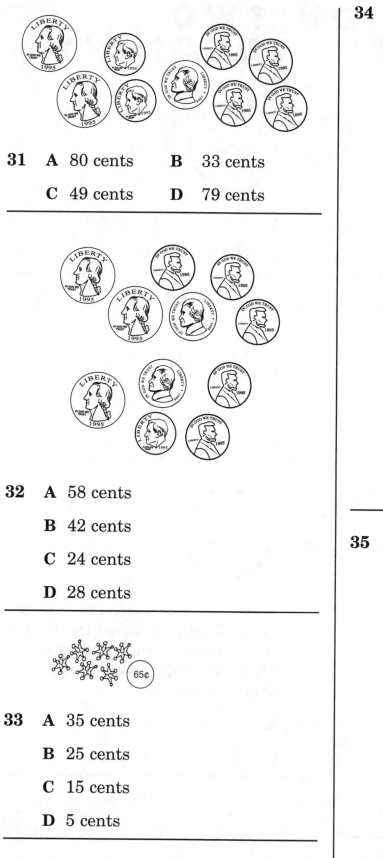

31 **A** 80 cents   **B** 33 cents

C 49 cents   **D** 79 cents

32 **A** 58 cents

B 42 cents

C 24 cents

D 28 cents

33 **A** 35 cents

B 25 cents

C 15 cents

D 5 cents

34 Look at the four groups of coins. Choose the group that has the most money.

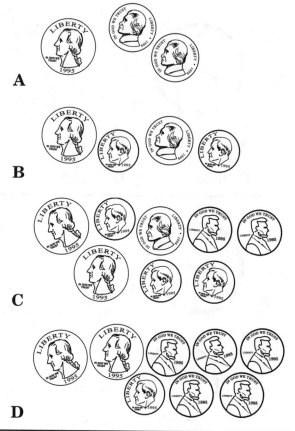

A

B

C

D

35 Adam wants to buy some football cards that cost $0.75 (75 cents). The picture shows how much money he has. How much more money does Adam need to buy cards?

A $0.20

B $0.25

C $0.10

D $0.15

GO

Cut along dashed line.

114

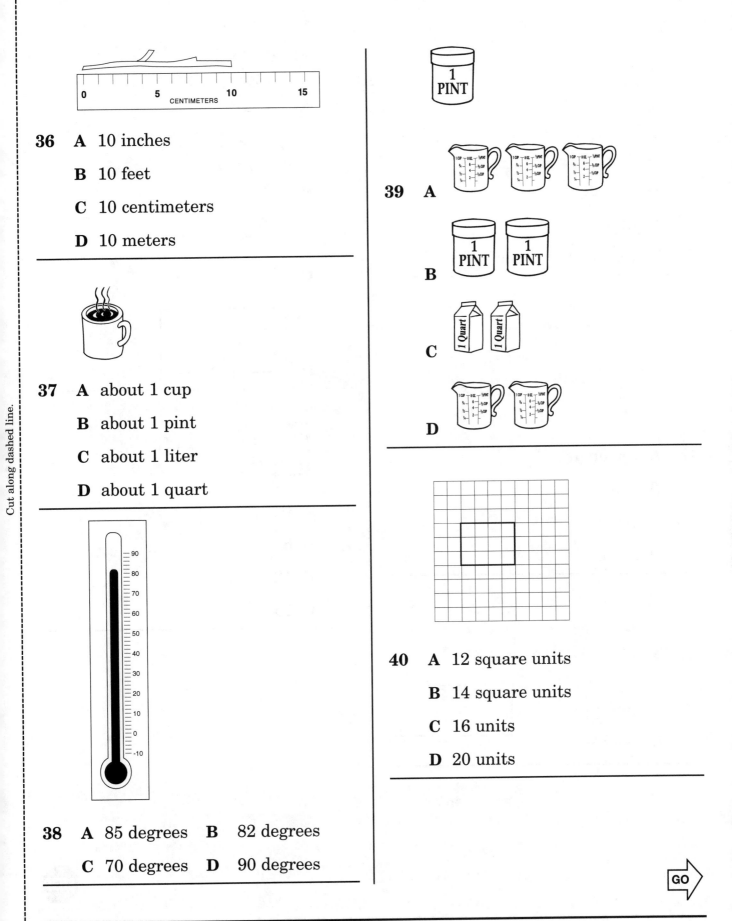

36 **A** 10 inches

B 10 feet

C 10 centimeters

D 10 meters

37 **A** about 1 cup

B about 1 pint

C about 1 liter

D about 1 quart

38 **A** 85 degrees   **B** 82 degrees

C 70 degrees   **D** 90 degrees

39 **A**

B

C

D

40 **A** 12 square units

B 14 square units

C 16 units

D 20 units

Cut along dashed line.

GO

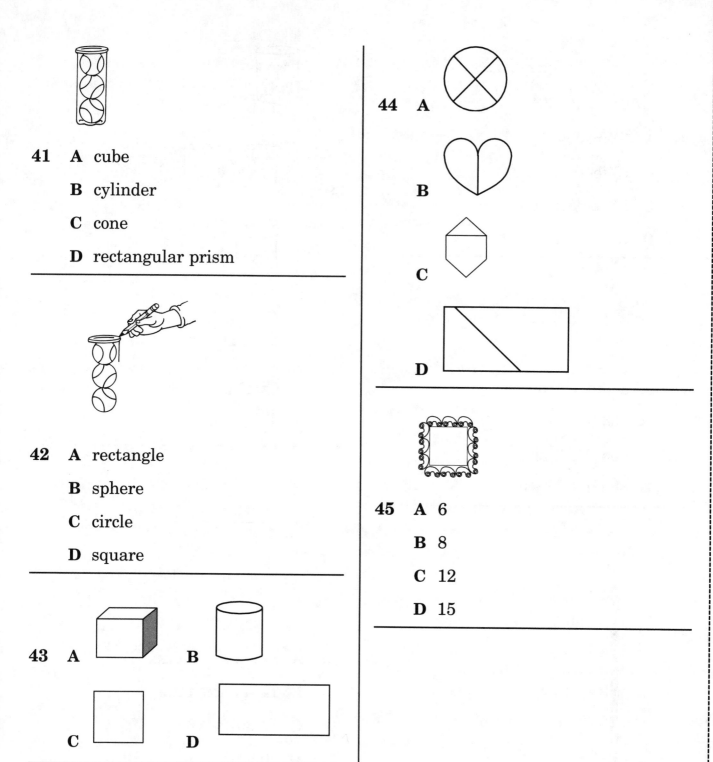

41 **A** cube

B cylinder

C cone

D rectangular prism

42 **A** rectangle

B sphere

C circle

D square

43 **A** **B**

C **D**

44 **A**

B

C

D

45 **A** 6

B 8

C 12

D 15

Cut along dashed line.

STOP

SESSION THREE
(STUDENT'S VERSION)

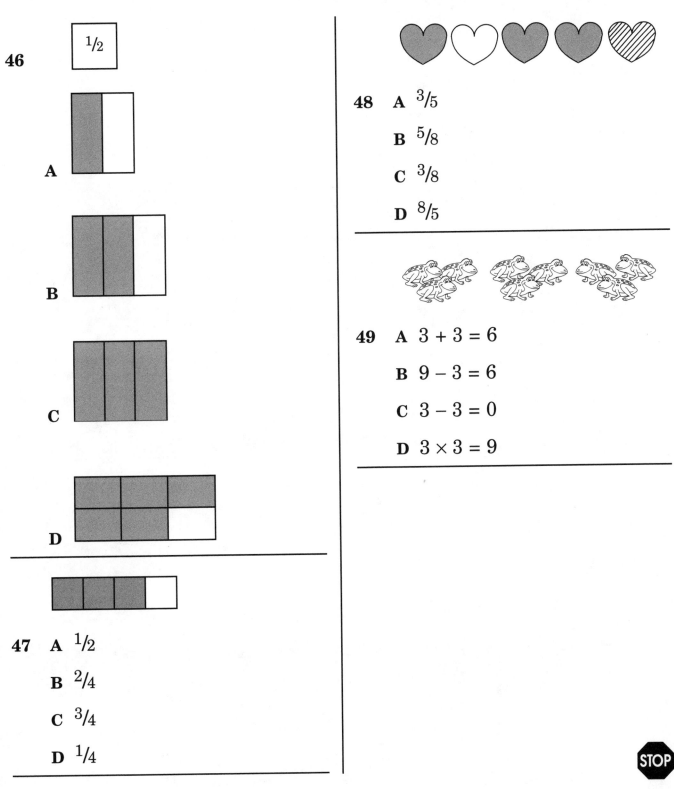

46

A

B

C

D

47 **A** $^1/_2$

B $^2/_4$

C $^3/_4$

D $^1/_4$

48 **A** $^3/_5$

B $^5/_8$

C $^3/_8$

D $^8/_5$

49 **A** $3 + 3 = 6$

B $9 - 3 = 6$

C $3 - 3 = 0$

D $3 \times 3 = 9$

Cut along dashed line.

STOP

Answer Key for Sample Practice Test

Session One

1	B
2	B
3	C
4	C
5	D
6	A
7	B
8	C
9	B
10	C
11	A
12	D

13	D
14	B
15	C
16	A
17	B
18	C
19	D
20	C
21	B
22	B
23	A
24	D
25	C

Session Two

26	B
27	C
28	C
29	A
30	A
31	D
32	B
33	A
34	C
35	D
36	C
37	A

38	B
39	D
40	A
41	B
42	C
43	B
44	B
45	C

Session Three

46	A
47	C
48	A
49	D